THE KIDS' BOOK OF
Number
Puzzles

Puzzles and solutions
by Dr. Gareth Moore
and Ellen Bailey

Illustrations by Nikalas Catlow
Edited by Ellen Bailey
Designed by Zoe Quayle
With thanks to Ariane Durkin
and Kate Byrne

Dr. Gareth Moore gained his PhD at Cambridge
University in the field of machine intelligence.
He is highly experienced in computer software
research and development, and produced his own
Kakuro creation software almost as soon as the first
puzzle appeared in a British newspaper. He has since
published *The Book of Kakuro: And How To Solve It,*
The Kids' Book of Kakuro, and *The Book of*
Japanese Puzzles: And How To Solve Them.
He has a wide range of media interests and has
written for both US and UK news-stand magazines. He
now runs his own video production company, Cantab
Films, and works on a range of puzzle and other
Web sites, including www.dokakuro.com
and www.dosudoku.com.

THE KIDS' BOOK OF
Number
Puzzles

simon
scribbles

New York London Toronto Sydney

An imprint of Simon & Schuster Children's Publishing Division
1230 Avenue of the Americas, New York, New York 10020

Sudoku, Kakuro, Hanjie, and Battleships puzzles and solutions
copyright © 2005 by Gareth Moore

Compilation and other puzzles and answers copyright © 2005 by
Buster Books

Originally published in Great Britain in 2005 by Buster Books,
an imprint of Michael O'Mara Books Limited.

SIMON SCRIBBLES and associated colophon are trademarks of
Simon & Schuster, Inc.

Manufactured in the United States of America

First Edition

10 9 8 7 6 5 4 3 2 1

ISBN-13: 978-1-4169-2733-4
ISBN-10: 1-4169-2733-6

Contents

Introduction

Are you a number-puzzle ninja ready for a number-puzzle challenge?

This book contains nine types of puzzles designed to test your skill, your cunning, and your determination. Can you master every kind and become a genuine number-puzzle genius?

Sudoku, Kakuro, Hanjie, and Battleships are seriously cool puzzles because they're simple to learn how to solve, but require intense logical thinking to complete. There are 25 of each of these puzzles in this book. The puzzles range in difficulty to put your talents to the test.

Dominoes, Number Searches, Crossnumbers, Towers, and Connectors are fierce brain-tickling puzzles. You will find 10 of each of these puzzles in this book.

Full of tips, tricks, and tactics, this book will make you a number-puzzling nemesis not to be messed with.

So what are you waiting for?

Daredevil Dominoes

Daredevil Dominoes

Are you Daredevil enough to take on the domino challenge? Arrange the dominoes so that the end of each one is touching a domino with the same number of dots. Choose the correct domino from the loose ones and copy the dots onto the empty dominoes to complete the puzzle.

Top Tip: Make sure you don't forget which dominoes you've already used by crossing them out as you go along.

puzzle 1

The answer to this puzzle is on page 198.

Daredevil Dominoes

puzzle 2

The answer to this puzzle
is on page 198.

9

Daredevil Dominoes

puzzle 3

The answer to this puzzle
is on page 199.

Daredevil
Dominoes

puzzle 4

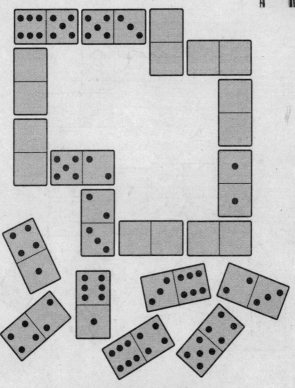

The answer to this puzzle
is on page 199.

Daredevil Dominoes

puzzle 5

The answer to this puzzle
is on page 200.

Daredevil Dominoes

puzzle 6

The answer to this puzzle
is on page 200.

Daredevil Dominoes

puzzle 7

The answer to this puzzle is on page 201.

14

Daredevil Dominoes

puzzle 8

The answer to this puzzle
is on page 201.

Daredevil Dominoes

puzzle 9

The answer to this puzzle
is on page 202.

Daredevil Dominoes

puzzle 10

The answer to this puzzle is on page 202.

Super-
Slammin'
Sudoku

How To Do Sudoku

The aim of Sudoku is to fill in all the missing numbers in a grid. A Sudoku grid consists of nine rows of nine squares, nine columns of nine squares, and nine boxes of nine squares. When a puzzle is complete, every column, row, and box must contain all the numbers from 1 to 9.

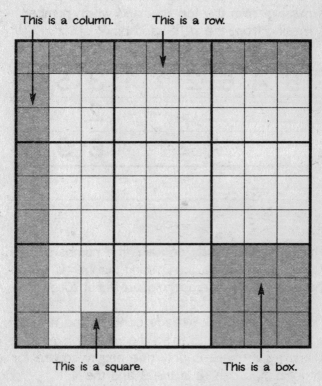

This is a column.   This is a row.

This is a square.   This is a box.

In every Sudoku puzzle some of the numbers in the grid have been filled in already. All you have to do is use logic to work out the numbers that go in each of the empty squares.

Getting Started

You don't need to be a mathematical genius to solve a Sudoku puzzle, you just need to be logical.

Remember that each row, box, and column needs to contain all the numbers from 1 to 9. Here is part of a Sudoku puzzle. Which number is missing from the top row and which number is missing from the right-hand box?

8	4	6	2		1	3	5	7
						2		1
						6	9	8

The top row already contains the numbers 1, 2, 3, 4, 5, 6, 7, and 8, so the missing number is 9, and there is only one empty square for it to go in.

The right-hand box already contains the numbers 1, 2, 3, 5, 6, 7, 8, and 9, so the missing number is 4, and again there is only one empty square for it to go in. You can fill in the 9 and the 4.

Easy, isn't it? Here are some tricks that will help you tackle the puzzles and turn you into a super Sudoku solver.

Tackling Trick One

In the example below, the boxes in the middle and on the right both already contain a 1. So where can 1 go in the left-hand box?

The top row already contains a 1, so no other square in that row can contain a 1.

The second row already contains a 1, so no other square in that row can contain a 1.

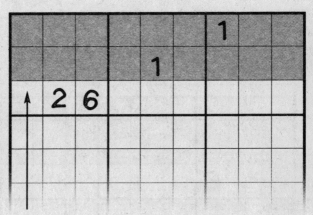

1 goes here.

This leaves just the third row and, as you can see, the third row in the left-hand box only has one empty square, so the missing number 1 must go in there.

See, you got your answer by a process of elimination. That means you decided where the 1 went by working out all the squares that it couldn't go in.

Tackling Trick Two

In the example below, the box in the middle and the box on the right both already contain a 1. So where can 1 go in the left-hand box?

The top row already contains a 1, so no other square in that row can contain a 1.

The second row already contains a 1, so no other square in that row can contain a 1.

This leaves the third row. You can see that there are two empty squares in this row in the left-hand box. So number 1 must go in one of these squares.

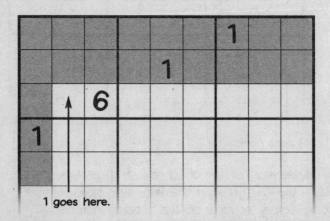

1 goes here.

Now look at the columns. If you look down the first column you can see that it contains a 1 already. So you know that 1 can't go in the first column of row three. The only place left is in the second column of row three.

Tackling Trick Three

In the example below, where does the 1 go in the right-hand box?

You know that another 1 cannot appear in any of the columns or rows that already contain a 1 (marked in gray).

Now look at the left-hand box. You know that number 1 in the left-hand box must appear in one of two squares (?) in its top row. This means that 1 cannot be in the top row in the right-hand box.

Now you can see that there is only one square in which the 1 can go in the right-hand box. Fill it in.

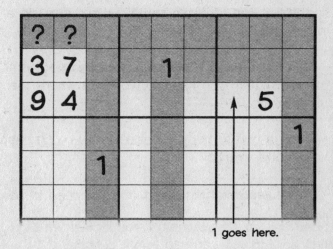

1 goes here.

And that's all there is to it! Are you ready? Then let's get Sudoku-ing . . .

Top Tips

• The puzzles get steadily harder as you work through the chapter, so start at the beginning.

• When you start a puzzle, look out for rows, columns, and boxes that have lots of numbers already filled in. It is often easy to complete these.

• Look for numbers that already appear frequently in the puzzle. See if more of these numbers can be filled in.

• When you place a number, it's a good idea to see if you can fill in the same number elsewhere in the grid.

• Never just guess a number. Every puzzle has all the information you need to work out where the numbers go.

• Trace a grid to copy a puzzle to if you find you have gone wrong.

• There is no math involved. You just need to be logical.

Good luck!

Super-Slammin' Sudoku

puzzle 11

7	6	1	2	3	4	8		5
8	9	5	6	1	7	3	2	4
4	2	3	5	8	9		7	6
9	8	4		2	3	5	6	7
	7	6	9		8	2	3	
3	1	2	7	6		4	8	9
6	4		8	5	2	7	1	3
2	3	7	4	9	1	6	5	8
1		8	3	7	6	9	4	2

The answer to this puzzle
is on page 203.

Super-Slammin' Sudoku

puzzle 12

		3	2	9	7	6	4	8
8	6	9	1	4	3	5	7	2
7	2	4	6		5	3	1	9
4	7	2	5	1		9	8	3
6	8	1	7		9	4	2	5
9	3	5		2	8	1	6	7
2	5	8	3		1	7	9	4
1	9	7	8	5	4	2	3	6
3	4	6	9	7	2	8		

The answer to this puzzle is on page 203.

Super-Slammin' Sudoku

puzzle 13

1	3	2		4		7	6	9
6	9	7	2	1	3	5	8	4
5	8	4	9	7	6	2	3	1
3		8	6	2		4	5	7
2	4	6	7		5	1	9	8
7	5	9		8	4	6		3
8	6	5	4	9	1	3	7	2
9	7	1	3	5	2	8	4	6
4	2	3		6		9	1	5

The answer to this puzzle is on page 203.

27

Super-Slammin' Sudoku

puzzle 14

3	9	6	7	5	1	4	8	2
8	5	7	9	2	4	6	3	1
2	4	1	6	3	8	9	7	5
1	8	5	3	6	9	7	2	4
6	7	3	1	4	2	5	9	8
9	2	4	8	7	5		6	
5	1	8	2	9		3	4	6
7	3	2	4	1	6	8		9
4	6	9	5	8	3	2	1	7

The answer to this puzzle is on page 204.

Super-Slammin' Sudoku

puzzle 15

3		9	5	1		8	7	2
8		5	3	2	7	9	4	6
4	2	7	9	6	8	1	3	5
5	4	6	8		2	3	1	7
2	7		6	4	1		9	8
9	8	1	7		5	6	2	4
1	5	8	2	7	3	4	6	9
6	3	2	4	8	9	7		1
7	9	4		5	6	2		3

The answer to this puzzle is on page 204.

Super-Slammin' Sudoku

puzzle 16

| 6 | 2 | 4 | 5 | 8 | | | 3 | 9 | 7 |

6	2	4	5	8		3	9	7
		1	2	7	6	8		
7	5	8	4	3	9	2	6	1
1	6	7	9	2	3		5	8
	4		6		7		3	
2	9		8	4	5	7	1	6
4	8	6	3	5	2	1	7	9
		9	7	6	8	5		
5	7	2		9	4	6	8	3

The answer to this puzzle
is on page 204.

Super-Slammin' Sudoku

puzzle 17

4	1	5	6	9	3		2	7
	2		5	1	8	4		3
8	3	6		4	2	1	9	5
			2	7		3	4	8
3	8	1	4	6	9	5	7	2
7	4	2		3	5			
2	9	8	1	5		7	3	6
1		3	9	8	6		5	
5	6		3	2	7	9	8	1

The answer to this puzzle
is on page 205.

Super-Slammin' Sudoku

puzzle 18

1			7	6	8	5	4	
7	5	3	4		1	6	8	9
4	6	8	5	9		7	1	2
6			1	5	7		2	8
8	2	1		3		9	5	7
3	7		2	8	9			1
9	1	4		7	6	2	3	5
5	3	6	9		2	8	7	4
	8	7	3	4	5			6

The answer to this puzzle
is on page 205.

Super-Slammin' Sudoku

puzzle 19

3	1	6	2	5	7	9	8	
8	7	9	3	4			6	2
4		2	9		8	1		3
5	2	3	7	1	6	8	4	
		8	5	3	9	7		
	9	7	8	2	4	3	5	1
7		1	4		2	6		5
9	6			7	5	2	3	8
	8	5	6	9	3	4	1	7

The answer to this puzzle
is on page 205.

Super-Slammin' Sudoku

puzzle 20

	1	9	4				6	5
5	6	7		9				4
2		3	7	6	5	1	9	8
1	2	4	6	3	7	5	8	9
3	8	5	9		4	6	2	7
7	9	6	2	5	8	3	4	1
4	3	8	5	7	2	9		6
6				4		8	5	2
9	5				6	4	7	

The answer to this puzzle
is on page 206.

Super-Slammin' Sudoku

puzzle 21

1	3	7	5			9	2	4
4					7		5	1
2		8		4	1	7	6	
3		1		9	4	6	7	5
7	4	5	1		8	3	9	2
9	2	6	7	3		4		8
	1	3	8	7		2		6
6	7		4					9
8	9	4			2	1	3	7

The answer to this puzzle is on page 206.

Super-Slammin' Sudoku

puzzle 22

			6	9	1			2
	6	5	8	7		1	9	4
1		2	4		3	6	8	7
	2		1		7	4	5	8
5	8	7	2		4	9	6	1
6	4	1	5		9		7	
8	1	9	7		5	3		6
2	3	6		1	8	7	4	
7			3	2	6			

The answer to this puzzle
is on page 206.

Super-Slammin' Sudoku

puzzle 23

7				9			8	2
2	6	4	3	8	1	5	7	
8		9	2		7	1		6
4	9	6	7	2				5
	2	8	5	1	9	6	4	
1				6	8	9	2	3
6		7	8		2	3		1
	3	1	9	7	4	2	6	8
9	8			3				4

The answer to this puzzle
is on page 207.

Super-Slammin' Sudoku

puzzle 24

6	8	7		4	1	5	2	3
2		3	6	5	7	1	4	8
5				2	8	7		
			1		6	7	4	
7	4		2		6		3	5
3	5	6		8				
		5	8	6				1
1	3	8	4	7	9	2		6
9	6	2	1	3		4	8	7

The answer to this puzzle is on page 207.

Super-Slammin' Sudoku

puzzle 25

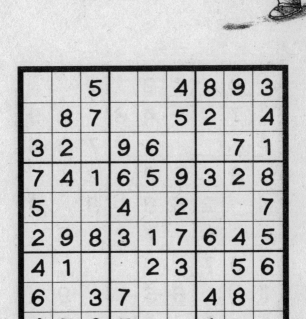

		5			4	8	9	3
	8	7			5	2		4
3	2		9	6			7	1
7	4	1	6	5	9	3	2	8
5			4		2			7
2	9	8	3	1	7	6	4	5
4	1			2	3		5	6
6		3	7			4	8	
8	7	2	5			1		

The answer to this puzzle
is on page 207.

Super-Slammin' Sudoku

puzzle 26

	4		7	2		1		
	7			4	6			9
						7	3	4
	8		6	9		2		
4		2	5	8	1	9		6
		6		7	2		8	
2	9	7						
1			8	5			9	
		3		6	9		1	

The answer to this puzzle
is on page 208.

Super-Slammin' Sudoku

puzzle 27

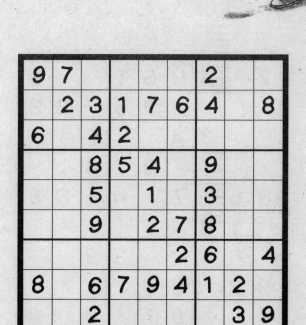

9	7					2		
8	2	3	1	7	6	4		8
6		4	2					
		8	5	4		9		
		5		1		3		
		9		2	7	8		
					2	6		4
8		6	7	9	4	1	2	
		2					3	9

The answer to this puzzle
is on page 208.

Super-Slammin' Sudoku

puzzle 28

2		4		3	1			6
				9	8		2	3
		3	4			5		
				8		3	1	
3	5		7		4		6	9
	1	8		5				
		6			3	9		
9	2		8	6				
4			9	7		6		8

The answer to this puzzle
is on page 208.

Super-Slammin' Sudoku

puzzle 29

1				9				8
	6		4	7	8		1	
2				5				
9	7	1	5				6	
6	8		1		9		3	5
	3				7	1	9	4
				4				3
	2		8	1	5		7	
8				6				1

The answer to this puzzle
is on page 209.

Super-Slammin' Sudoku

puzzle 30

		8	4		1			7
				9		4		8
		4	3				5	
2	8			6		3		
6	9	3		7		8	2	5
		7		8			9	6
		6			5	9		
7		9		3				
5			9		6	7		

The answer to this puzzle
is on page 209.

Super-Slammin' Sudoku

puzzle 31

				8		6	2	1
						3		
8		3	6	2		9	5	
6	2	8	4					
		7				2		
					2	7	8	9
	5	2		1	3	4		6
		1						
9	8	4		5				

The answer to this puzzle
is on page 209.

Super-Slammin' Sudoku

puzzle 32

				2		3	6	
			9	5		7		
9		6			8			2
1		2		9		4	3	7
7	9	5		6		2		1
2			5			6		3
		7		4	3			
	5	8		7				

The answer to this puzzle
is on page 210.

Super-Slammin' Sudoku

puzzle 33

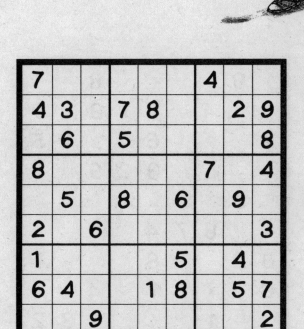

7						4		
4	3		7	8			2	9
	6		5					8
8						7		4
	5		8		6		9	
2		6						3
1					5		4	
6	4			1	8		5	7
		9						2

The answer to this puzzle is on page 210.

Super-Slammin' Sudoku

puzzle 34

1	6					8		
		4		5	1	3		9
9				6			1	5
				3	2	9		
	3						4	
		8	7	4				
3	2			8				1
6		7	2	1		4		
		1					3	2

The answer to this puzzle
is on page 210.

Super-Slammin' Sudoku

puzzle 35

		9		5		7	6	
	8	6			3			
5	1				6		4	
		3	6		9	5		7
6		7	4		8	3		
	6		3				5	2
			7			9	1	
8	7		5		1			

The answer to this puzzle
is on page 210.

Nail-Biting Number Searches

Nail-Biting Number Searches

Can you use your skill and cunning to find the numbers hidden in the grids? They might be arranged horizontally, vertically, or diagonally. You'd better prepare yourself — solving these puzzles will take all your number-ninja powers!

puzzle 3 6

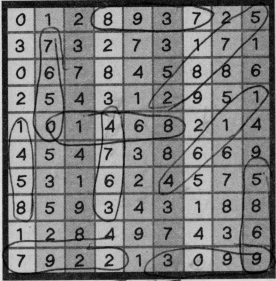

0	1	2	8	9	3	7	2	5
3	7	3	2	7	3	1	7	1
0	6	7	8	4	5	8	8	6
2	5	4	3	1	2	9	5	1
1	0	1	4	6	8	2	1	4
4	5	4	7	3	8	6	6	9
5	3	1	6	2	4	5	7	5
8	5	9	3	4	3	1	8	8
1	2	8	4	9	7	4	3	6
7	9	2	2	1	3	0	9	9

1468	8541
8937	2237
7660	4798
2875	9685
3099	1184

The answer to this puzzle is on page 211.

51

Nail-Biting Number Searches

puzzle 37

3	3	5	6	4	5	9	3	4
2	1	6	4	8	7	8	2	8
1	2	9	3	4	9	6	1	5
3	3	4	6	2	6	5	7	2
5	8	5	8	7	9	2	4	2
3	7	2	9	4	5	6	3	1
1	9	4	9	6	7	8	1	2
6	3	9	1	7	3	5	6	3
9	6	6	5	0	7	6	4	8
5	1	9	8	4	1	2	4	6

2568	2584
5699	7546
1246	9986
6572	5961
3356	2387

The answer to this puzzle is on page 211.

Nail-Biting Number Searches

puzzle 38

3	4	8	6	4	5	9	5	2
1	6	4	6	8	3	2	1	2
9	9	4	9	7	2	6	6	3
3	7	2	3	9	7	1	8	6
6	9	8	2	4	8	5	2	3
6	1	7	8	7	1	4	6	9
8	2	2	4	6	7	3	5	7
5	5	3	4	5	3	2	4	8
7	4	9	1	2	4	8	6	3
9	8	3	5	2	8	9	4	1

2894	5468
5464	6693
2236	4751
5489	1254
6685	6187

The answer to this puzzle is on page 211.

Nail-Biting Number Searches

puzzle 39

1	1	2	5	3	1	3	6	3
9	3	2	4	5	7	1	3	4
1	3	5	6	4	2	5	8	5
9	4	6	5	9	7	3	2	6
8	3	9	2	6	4	8	3	1
7	2	9	4	8	3	9	5	7
6	8	9	5	3	2	2	1	8
7	5	6	4	4	1	3	5	8
2	7	8	3	8	7	6	4	5
6	1	2	4	6	9	1	4	4

5642	5467
9965	6392
4588	1125
1246	6789
3357	5644

The answer to this puzzle
is on page 211.

Nail-Biting Number Searches

puzzle 40

6	6	4	5	3	1	4	9	5
5	3	7	3	2	4	6	5	8
2	9	4	3	8	9	7	6	4
1	6	8	6	3	2	2	3	6
2	5	1	4	6	7	8	4	9
4	2	4	8	9	4	5	7	8
9	5	9	4	4	1	1	8	3
8	7	6	2	3	4	6	5	8
1	8	9	8	4	3	9	3	9
9	2	5	7	6	2	5	8	7

5846	6645
2236	9514
9864	3648
2587	2465
5693	8942

The answer to this puzzle is on page 212.

Nail-Biting Number Searches

puzzle 41

9	2	1	9	3	1	6	8	1
1	4	8	9	6	3	6	2	1
6	2	5	3	2	7	4	5	3
3	1	8	4	9	8	5	9	5
2	8	6	2	3	5	9	2	1
9	3	7	5	6	4	7	9	5
4	2	4	7	5	6	2	8	8
7	6	5	4	1	5	2	6	3
6	1	9	8	5	8	6	2	2
4	8	7	7	6	5	9	7	4

2359	5832
7854	6749
8622	3526
4697	9934
1135	8771

The answer to this puzzle
is on page 212.

Nail-Biting Number Searches

puzzle 42

3	2	6	3	6	1	9	8	1
9	4	7	1	4	6	6	7	2
8	7	5	2	3	2	4	5	3
4	2	8	3	5	6	2	8	8
3	2	2	6	4	2	5	5	7
7	3	4	1	8	6	6	9	6
1	8	6	9	7	5	3	4	2
5	1	2	6	5	3	2	9	7
4	3	1	5	9	3	2	1	9
2	4	4	6	9	8	6	5	7

6672	5621
3984	7972
2516	8669
4875	4318
9123	1365

The answer to this puzzle is on page 212.

Nail-Biting Number Searches

puzzle 43

5	4	3	4	4	8	6	2	6
4	1	6	9	2	4	1	8	2
8	2	1	9	7	6	7	1	3
1	3	1	6	3	2	9	5	6
8	5	9	4	1	8	3	3	7
5	5	7	6	2	4	6	5	2
9	2	4	7	5	8	7	3	1
3	6	9	7	3	1	1	8	4
8	2	1	3	6	8	7	9	6
9	1	5	7	2	5	3	9	7

3128	7911
4652	8443
8197	2972
5576	1976
6236	1845

The answer to this puzzle
is on page 213.

Nail-Biting Number Searches

puzzle 44

3	5	1	3	4	5	1	8	4
7	2	8	6	2	7	8	6	2
1	5	7	4	3	6	7	1	6
6	8	3	2	1	9	5	4	3
7	7	2	5	4	3	8	7	9
8	2	4	6	1	6	5	2	2
2	4	1	6	6	8	7	3	8
4	9	4	1	4	5	5	9	1
6	8	3	5	7	3	9	4	6
4	2	8	1	2	6	7	1	4

4367	8758
9281	7346
6659	4815
2876	1824
1423	3272

The answer to this puzzle
is on page 213.

Nail-Biting Number Searches

puzzle 45

3	5	7	6	7	9	1	4	3
1	7	8	4	4	7	9	4	2
3	1	2	9	4	5	3	4	2
2	5	3	1	2	9	8	8	8
1	6	5	9	8	4	3	3	4
1	6	8	6	4	1	9	2	2
4	4	5	1	3	2	4	6	5
8	9	6	4	6	3	7	8	9
3	5	1	7	9	4	5	7	1
8	8	6	2	2	3	3	8	3

3576	5946
6491	6942
7629	3211
3383	8862
4483	2482

The answer to this puzzle is on page 213.

Kickin' Kakuro

How To Do Kakuro

In all Kakuro puzzles, like the one below, you will see white squares, gray squares, and darker gray squares. The aim of Kakuro is to fill each white square with a single number from 1 to 9.

The white squares appear in rows or columns called **runs**. Runs can vary in length — in the example below they are two or three squares long. A run stops when it reaches a non-white square.

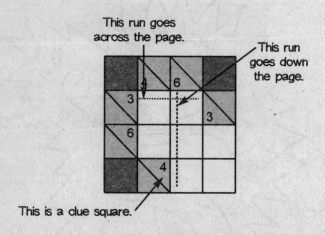

This run goes across the page.

This run goes down the page.

This is a clue square.

The gray squares are called **clue** squares, because they contain number clues that will help you solve the Kakuro puzzle. The clues are written either above or below a diagonal line.

These clues tell you what the total will be if all the numbers in a run are added up.

If a clue number appears above the diagonal line it is the total of the run to its right. If it appears below the diagonal line, then it gives the total of the run directly below the clue. It works like this:

This is the total of the run going across the page.

This is the total of the run going down the page.

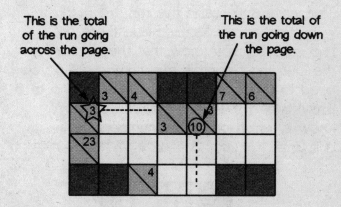

Getting Started

Remember, the aim of Kakuro is to fit numbers into all of the white squares. To do this you need to work out which numbers add up to the totals shown in the clue squares. You can only use the numbers 1 to 9.

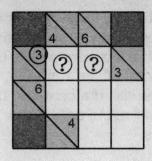

Look at the clue '3' circled in this picture. The white squares in this run are marked with question marks. Because there are two squares, you know that the solution to the clue must contain two numbers. So you need to find two numbers which add up to 3. Easy! $3 = 1 + 2$, right? What you don't know is which order the numbers go in. Is it $3 = 1 + 2$ or $3 = 2 + 1$?

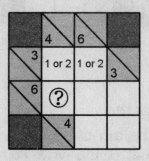

Look at the square with the question mark. You know from the clue that this square and the square above it need to add up to 4.

Again there are two squares in this run, and this time you need to find two numbers that add up to 4. There seem to be two possibilities, either $1 + 3 = 4$, or $2 + 2 = 4$. But there's a very important rule in Kakuro:

You cannot, EVER, repeat the same number within a run.

This means that you can't use $2 + 2 = 4$ because this would mean repeating the number 2. So the two numbers that you need to solve the clue '4' are 1 and 3.

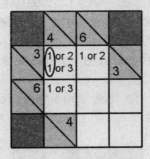

You now know that you can only solve this clue with either $1 + 3$ or $3 + 1$. However, look at the '1 or 2' written in the top-left square. You already know this square can't contain a 3, so it can only be 1.

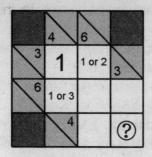

Now you can solve the other two squares you've written '1 or 2' and '1 or 3' in, and write in 2 and 3.

Look at where the question mark is now in the grid above. This is just like the square you put the 1 into. This square with the question mark has to be a number which is in the solution for both the clue '3' and the clue '4'. You should be able to solve this the same way as you just worked out the number 1 above. If you do this you'll then have a grid that looks like this:

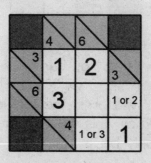

Nearly done! Now you can write in the 2 and 3 using the same logic as before. This just leaves the middle white square marked below with a question mark:

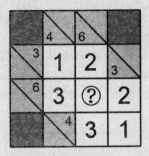

Here you have 6 = 3 + ? + 2 reading across, and 6 = 2 + ? + 3 reading down. Well, you know that 6 = 3 + 1 + 2, just as 6 = 2 + 1 + 3 too — so the across and down clues both have 1 as the middle number.

Write it in to finish the grid. That's all there is to it!

Here are some extra tricks that will turn you into a true Kakuro king:

Tackling Trick One

If a number only fits in one square, it must go there. Say you're trying to work out where 1, 2, and 3 go in a clue run to make a total of 6, and you have some possibilities like the ones shown below for each of the three squares:

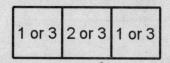

You can work out that the 2 goes in the middle square because you know that there must be a 2 in the answer, and there is only one square it can fit in.

Tackling Trick Two

Say you're trying to solve a clue with four squares in its run and a clue total of 10. Imagine you have the following options:

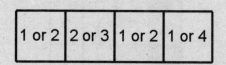

You know that the only possible solution to the clue '10' is $1 + 2 + 3 + 4$, so you have to have both a 1 and a 2. Because the first and third squares can only contain 1 or 2, they cannot also go in the second or fourth squares. Now you can cross out 1 and 2 from these squares to leave just 3 in the second square and 4 in the last.

Top Tips

• The puzzles get steadily harder as you work through the chapter, so start at the beginning.

• If you use a pencil to write in the possible numbers that might fit in each square, you'll find it much easier to solve the puzzles. Don't forget to cross out the used numbers as you go.

Marvelous Math

The following lists show all the sums you need to solve the Kakuro puzzles in this book. Count how many squares there are in the run you're trying to solve and pick the matching table. Look up the clue total on the left-hand side of the table to find out which number combinations can be used to make up that total.

Runs of Length 2:

3:	1,2;
4:	1,3;
5:	1,4; 2,3;
6:	1,5; 2,4;
7:	1,6; 2,5; 3,4;
8:	1,7; 2,6; 3,5;
9:	1,8; 2,7; 3,6; 4,5;
10:	1,9; 2,8; 3,7; 4,6;
11:	2,9; 3,8; 4,7; 5,6;
12:	3,9; 4,8; 5,7;
13:	4,9; 5,8; 6,7;
14:	5,9; 6,8;
15:	6,9; 7,8;
16:	7,9;
17:	8,9;

Runs of Length 3:

6:	1,2,3;
7:	1,2,4;
8:	1,2,5; 1,3,4;
9:	1,2,6; 1,3,5; 2,3,4;
10:	1,2,7; 1,3,6; 1,4,5; 2,3,5;
11:	1,2,8; 1,3,7; 1,4,6; 2,3,6; 2,4,5;
12:	1,2,9; 1,3,8; 1,4,7; 1,5,6; 2,3,7; 2,4,6; 3,4,5;
13:	1,3,9; 1,4,8; 1,5,7; 2,3,8; 2,4,7; 2,5,6; 3,4,6;
14:	1,4,9; 1,5,8; 1,6,7; 2,3,9; 2,4,8; 2,5,7; 3,4,7; 3,5,6;
15:	1,5,9; 1,6,8; 2,4,9; 2,5,8; 2,6,7; 3,4,8; 3,5,7; 4,5,6;
16:	1,6,9; 1,7,8; 2,5,9; 2,6,8; 3,4,9; 3,5,8; 3,6,7; 4,5,7;
17:	1,7,9; 2,6,9; 2,7,8; 3,5,9; 3,6,8; 4,5,8; 4,6,7;
18:	1,8,9; 2,7,9; 3,6,9; 3,7,8; 4,5,9; 4,6,8; 5,6,7;
19:	2,8,9; 3,7,9; 4,6,9; 4,7,8; 5,6,8;
20:	3,8,9; 4,7,9; 5,6,9; 5,7,8;
21:	4,8,9; 5,7,9; 6,7,8;
22:	5,8,9; 6,7,9;
23:	6,8,9;
24:	7,8,9;

Runs of Length 4:

10: 1,2,3,4;

11: 1,2,3,5;

12: 1,2,3,6; 1,2,4,5;

13: 1,2,3,7; 1,2,4,6; 1,3,4,5;

14: 1,2,3,8; 1,2,4,7; 1,2,5,6; 1,3,4,6; 2,3,4,5;

15: 1,2,3,9; 1,2,4,8; 1,2,5,7; 1,3,4,7; 1,3,5,6; 2,3,4,6;

16: 1,2,4,9; 1,2,5,8; 1,2,6,7; 1,3,4,8; 1,3,5,7; 1,4,5,6; 2,3,4,7; 2,3,5,6;

17: 1,2,5,9; 1,2,6,8; 1,3,4,9; 1,3,5,8; 1,3,6,7; 1,4,5,7; 2,3,4,8; 2,3,5,7; 2,4,5,6;

18: 1,2,6,9; 1,2,7,8; 1,3,5,9; 1,3,6,8; 1,4,5,8; 1,4,6,7; 2,3,4,9; 2,3,5,8; 2,3,6,7; 2,4,5,7; 3,4,5,6;

19: 1,2,7,9; 1,3,6,9; 1,3,7,8; 1,4,5,9; 1,4,6,8; 1,5,6,7; 2,3,5,9; 2,3,6,8; 2,4,5,8; 2,4,6,7; 3,4,5,7;

20: 1,2,8,9; 1,3,7,9; 1,4,6,9; 1,4,7,8; 1,5,6,8; 2,3,6,9; 2,3,7,8; 2,4,5,9; 2,4,6,8; 2,5,6,7; 3,4,5,8; 3,4,6,7;

21: 1,3,8,9; 1,4,7,9; 1,5,6,9; 1,5,7,8; 2,3,7,9; 2,4,6,9; 2,4,7,8; 2,5,6,8; 3,4,5,9; 3,4,6,8; 3,5,6,7;

22: 1,4,8,9; 1,5,7,9; 1,6,7,8; 2,3,8,9; 2,4,7,9; 2,5,6,9; 2,5,7,8; 3,4,6,9; 3,4,7,8; 3,5,6,8; 4,5,6,7;

23: 1,5,8,9; 1,6,7,9; 2,4,8,9; 2,5,7,9; 2,6,7,8; 3,4,7,9; 3,5,6,9; 3,5,7,8; 4,5,6,8;

24: 1,6,8,9; 2,5,8,9; 2,6,7,9; 3,4,8,9; 3,5,7,9; 3,6,7,8; 4,5,6,9; 4,5,7,8;

25: 1,7,8,9; 2,6,8,9; 3,5,8,9; 3,6,7,9; 4,5,7,9; 4,6,7,8;

26: 2,7,8,9; 3,6,8,9; 4,5,8,9; 4,6,7,9; 5,6,7,8;

27: 3,7,8,9; 4,6,8,9; 5,6,7,9;

28: 4,7,8,9; 5,6,8,9;

29: 5,7,8,9;

30: 6,7,8,9;

Runs of Length 5:

15: 1,2,3,4,5;

16: 1,2,3,4,6;

17: 1,2,3,4,7; 1,2,3,5,6;

18: 1,2,3,4,8; 1,2,3,5,7; 1,2,4,5,6;

19: 1,2,3,4,9; 1,2,3,5,8; 1,2,3,6,7; 1,2,4,5,7; 1,3,4,5,6;

20: 1,2,3,5,9; 1,2,3,6,8; 1,2,4,5,8; 1,2,4,6,7; 1,3,4,5,7; 2,3,4,5,6;

21: 1,2,3,6,9; 1,2,3,7,8; 1,2,4,5,9; 1,2,4,6,8; 1,2,5,6,7; 1,3,4,5,8; 1,3,4,6,7; 2,3,4,5,7;

22: 1,2,3,7,9; 1,2,4,6,9; 1,2,4,7,8; 1,2,5,6,8; 1,3,4,5,9; 1,3,4,6,8; 1,3,5,6,7; 2,3,4,5,8; 2,3,4,6,7;

23: 1,2,3,8,9; 1,2,4,7,9; 1,2,5,6,9; 1,2,5,7,8; 1,3,4,6,9; 1,3,4,7,8; 1,3,5,6,8; 1,4,5,6,7; 2,3,4,5,9; 2,3,4,6,8; 2,3,5,6,7;

24: 1,2,4,8,9; 1,2,5,7,9; 1,2,6,7,8; 1,3,4,7,9; 1,3,5,6,9; 1,3,5,7,8; 1,4,5,6,8; 2,3,4,6,9; 2,3,4,7,8; 2,3,5,6,8; 2,4,5,6,7;

25: 1,2,5,8,9; 1,2,6,7,9; 1,3,4,8,9; 1,3,5,7,9; 1,3,6,7,8; 1,4,5,6,9; 1,4,5,7,8; 2,3,4,7,9; 2,3,5,6,9; 2,3,5,7,8; 2,4,5,6,8; 3,4,5,6,7;

26: 1,2,6,8,9; 1,3,5,8,9; 1,3,6,7,9; 1,4,5,7,9; 1,4,6,7,8; 2,3,4,8,9; 2,3,5,7,9; 2,3,6,7,8; 2,4,5,6,9; 2,4,5,7,8; 3,4,5,6,8;

27: 1,2,7,8,9; 1,3,6,8,9; 1,4,5,8,9; 1,4,6,7,9; 1,5,6,7,8; 2,3,5,8,9; 2,3,6,7,9; 2,4,5,7,9; 2,4,6,7,8; 3,4,5,6,9; 3,4,5,7,8;

28: 1,3,7,8,9; 1,4,6,8,9; 1,5,6,7,9; 2,3,6,8,9; 2,4,5,8,9; 2,4,6,7,9; 2,5,6,7,8; 3,4,5,7,9; 3,4,6,7,8;

29: 1,4,7,8,9; 1,5,6,8,9; 2,3,7,8,9; 2,4,6,8,9; 2,5,6,7,9; 3,4,5,8,9; 3,4,6,7,9; 3,5,6,7,8;

30: 1,5,7,8,9; 2,4,7,8,9; 2,5,6,8,9; 3,4,6,8,9; 3,5,6,7,9; 4,5,6,7,8;

31: 1,6,7,8,9; 2,5,7,8,9; 3,4,7,8,9; 3,5,6,8,9; 4,5,6,7,9;

32: 2,6,7,8,9; 3,5,7,8,9; 4,5,6,8,9;

33: 3,6,7,8,9; 4,5,7,8,9;

34: 4,6,7,8,9;

35: 5,6,7,8,9;

Runs of Length 6:

21: 1.2.3.4.5.6;

22: 1.2.3.4.5.7;

23: 1.2.3.4.5.8; 1.2.3.4.6.7;

24: 1.2.3.4.5.9; 1.2.3.4.6.8; 1.2.3.5.6.7;

25: 1.2.3.4.6.9; 1.2.3.4.7.8; 1.2.3.5.6.8; 1.2.4.5.6.7;

26: 1.2.3.4.7.9; 1.2.3.5.6.9; 1.2.3.5.7.8; 1.2.4.5.6.8; 1.3.4.5.6.7;

27: 1.2.3.4.8.9; 1.2.3.5.7.9; 1.2.3.6.7.8; 1.2.4.5.6.9; 1.2.4.5.7.8; 1.3.4.5.6.8; 2.3.4.5.6.7;

28: 1.2.3.5.8.9; 1.2.3.6.7.9; 1.2.4.5.7.9; 1.2.4.6.7.8; 1.3.4.5.6.9; 1.3.4.5.7.8; 2.3.4.5.6.8;

29: 1.2.3.6.8.9; 1.2.4.5.8.9; 1.2.4.6.7.9; 1.2.5.6.7.8; 1.3.4.5.7.9; 1.3.4.6.7.8; 2.3.4.5.6.9; 2.3.4.5.7.8;

30: 1.2.3.7.8.9; 1.2.4.6.8.9; 1.2.5.6.7.9; 1.3.4.5.8.9; 1.3.4.6.7.9; 1.3.5.6.7.8; 2.3.4.5.7.9; 2.3.4.6.7.8;

31: 1.2.4.7.8.9; 1.2.5.6.8.9; 1.3.4.6.8.9; 1.3.5.6.7.9; 1.4.5.6.7.8; 2.3.4.5.8.9; 2.3.4.6.7.9; 2.3.5.6.7.8;

32: 1.2.5.7.8.9; 1.3.4.7.8.9; 1.3.5.6.8.9; 1.4.5.6.7.9; 2.3.4.6.8.9; 2.3.5.6.7.9; 2.4.5.6.7.8;

33: 1.2.6.7.8.9; 1.3.5.7.8.9; 1.4.5.6.8.9; 2.3.4.7.8.9; 2.3.5.6.8.9; 2.4.5.6.7.9; 3.4.5.6.7.8;

34: 1.3.6.7.8.9; 1.4.5.7.8.9; 2.3.5.7.8.9; 2.4.5.6.8.9; 3.4.5.6.7.9;

35: 1.4.6.7.8.9; 2.3.6.7.8.9; 2.4.5.7.8.9; 3.4.5.6.8.9;

36: 1.5.6.7.8.9; 2.4.6.7.8.9; 3.4.5.7.8.9;

37: 2.5.6.7.8.9; 3.4.6.7.8.9;

38: 3.5.6.7.8.9;

39: 4.5.6.7.8.9;

Kickin' Kakuro

puzzle 46

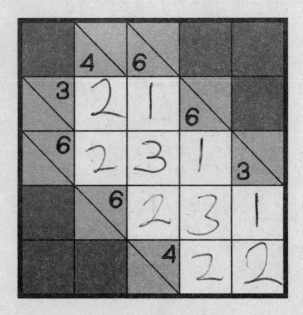

The answer to this puzzle is on page 214.

74

Kickin' Kakuro

puzzle 47

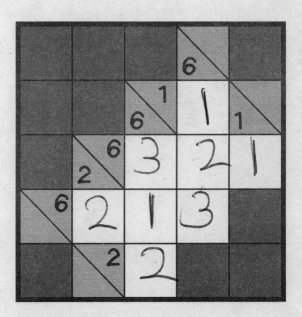

The answer to this puzzle
is on page 214.

Kickin' Kakuro

puzzle 48

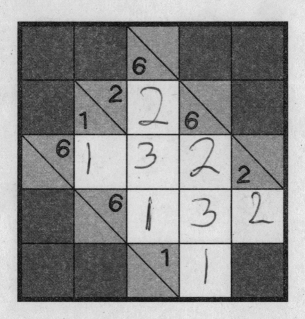

The answer to this puzzle is on page 215.

Kickin' Kakuro

puzzle 49

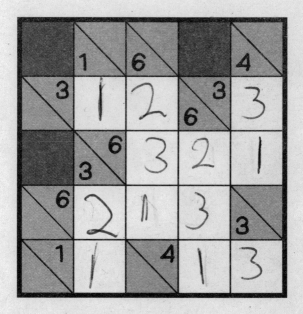

The answer to this puzzle
is on page 215.

Kickin' Kakuro

puzzle 50

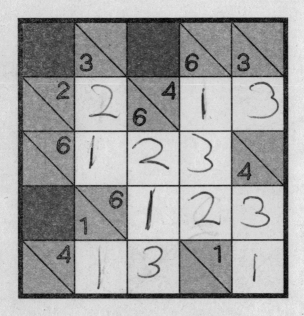

The answer to this puzzle is on page 216.

Kickin' Kakuro

puzzle 51

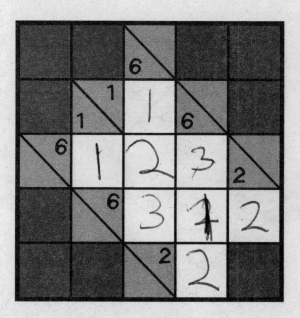

The answer to this puzzle
is on page 216.

Kickin' Kakuro

puzzle 52

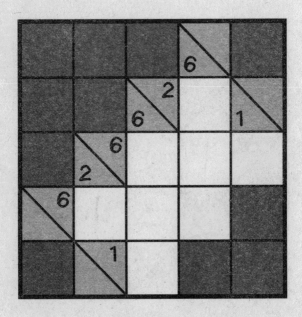

The answer to this puzzle is on page 217.

Kickin' Kakuro

puzzle 53

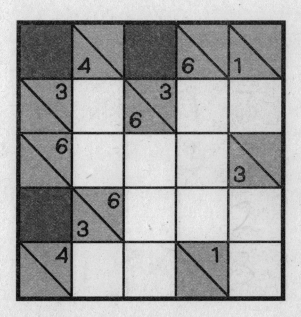

The answer to this puzzle
is on page 217.

Kickin' Kakuro

puzzle 54

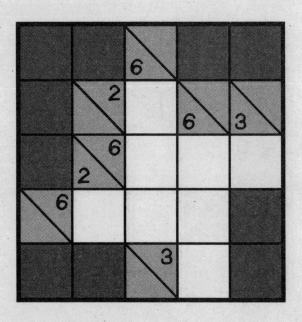

The answer to this puzzle is on page 218.

puzzle 55

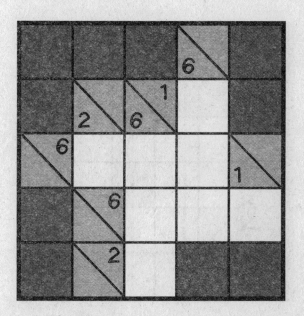

The answer to this puzzle
is on page 218.

Kickin' Kakuro

puzzle 56

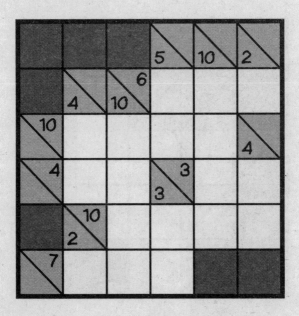

The answer to this puzzle
is on page 219.

Kickin' Kakuro

puzzle 57

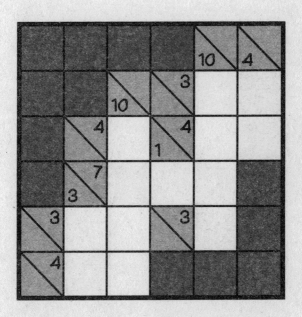

The answer to this puzzle
is on page 219.

Kickin' Kakuro

puzzle 58

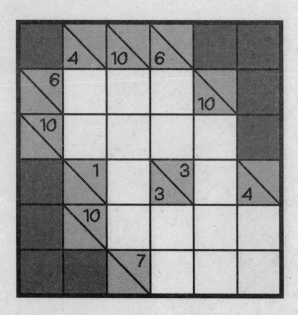

The answer to this puzzle
is on page 220.

Kickin' Kakuro

puzzle 59

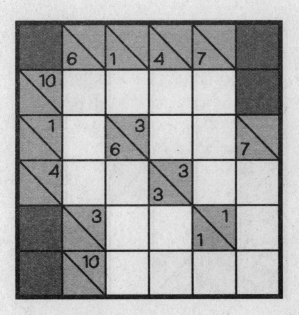

The answer to this puzzle
is on page 220.

Kickin' Kakuro

puzzle 60

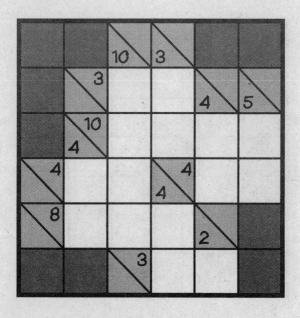

The answer to this puzzle is on page 221.

Kickin' Kakuro

puzzle 61

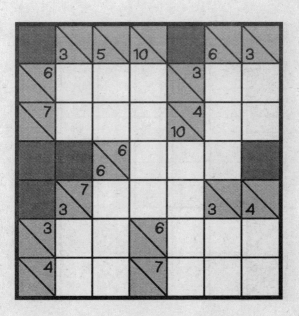

The answer to this puzzle is on page 221.

Kickin' Kakuro

puzzle 62

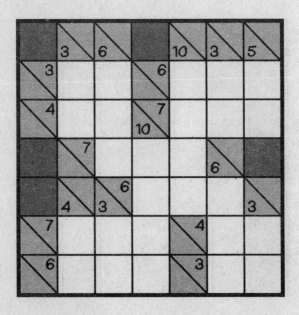

The answer to this puzzle
is on page 222.

Kickin' Kakuro

puzzle 63

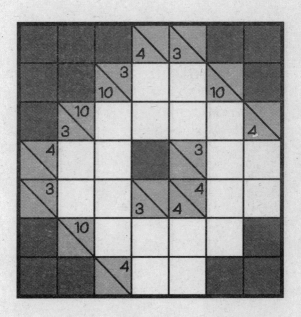

The answer to this puzzle
is on page 222.

Kickin' Kakuro

puzzle 64

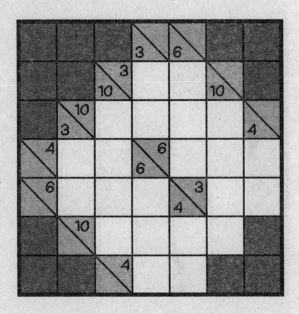

The answer to this puzzle is on page 223.

Kickin' Kakuro

puzzle 65

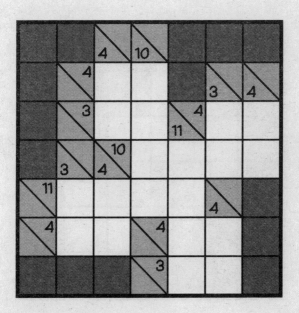

The answer to this puzzle
is on page 223.

Kickin' Kakuro

puzzle 66

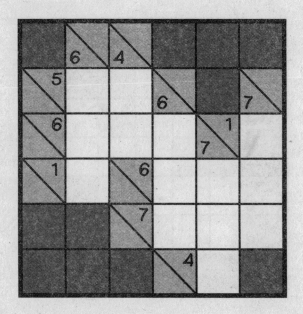

The answer to this puzzle is on page 224.

Kickin' Kakuro

puzzle 67

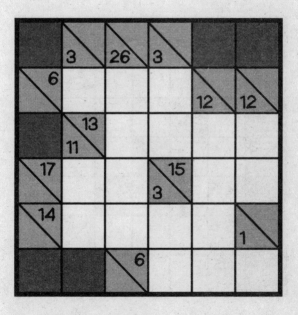

The answer to this puzzle is on page 224.

Kickin' Kakuro

puzzle 68

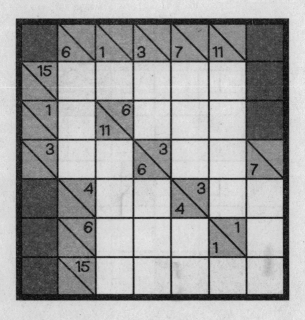

The answer to this puzzle is on page 225.

Kickin' Kakuro

puzzle 69

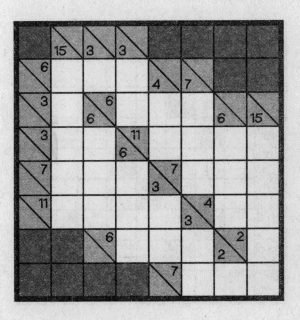

The answer to this puzzle
is on page 225.

97

Kickin' Kakuro

puzzle 70

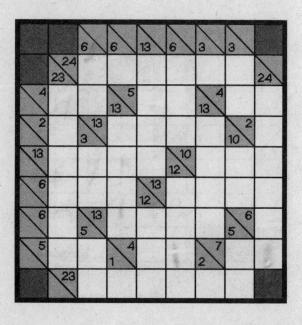

The answer to this puzzle
is on page 225.

Cool
Crossnumbers

Cool Crossnumbers

Cross*numbers* are just like cross*words* except that, well, there aren't any words!

Below each grid you will find two sets of clues — one set for answers that go ACROSS the grid, and one set for answers that go DOWN the grid.

1 down.

1 across.

To complete the puzzle work out the answer to each clue then place it in the corresponding boxes in the grid.

Have a look at the puzzle on the opposite page. Clue 1 ACROSS is 'one hundred and one'. Look for the little number '1' in the grid — you can see that the answer to this clue goes in the three boxes across the top left. To fit in the grid the answer needs to be written '101'. Fill it in.

Now look at the clue for 1 DOWN. It is 12x12. If you look at the grid you can see that the answer begins with a 1. Can you work out the rest?

Cool Crossnumbers

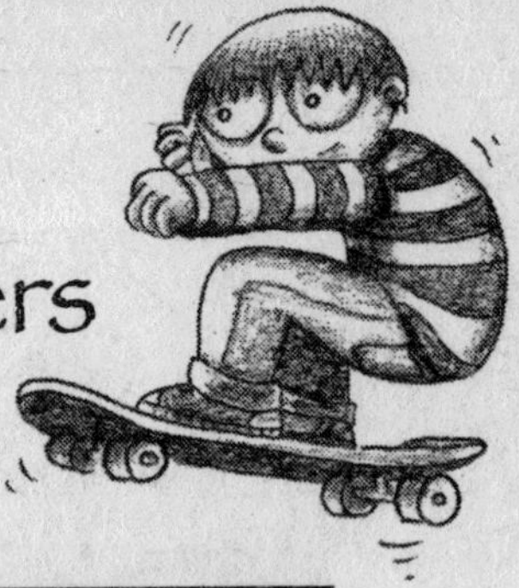

puzzle 71

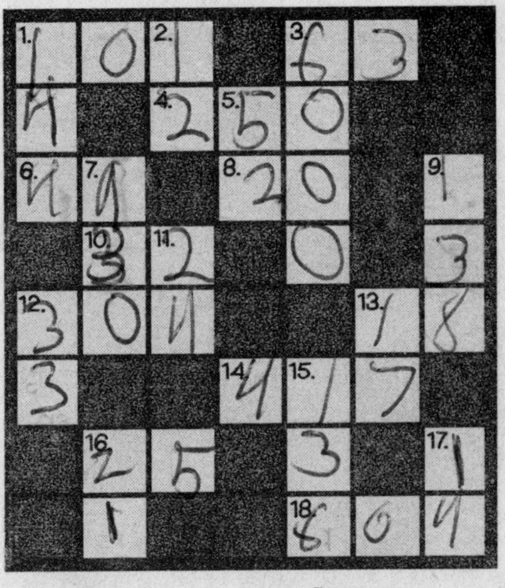

Across

1. One hundred and one
3. 9x7
4. 200+50
6. 55-6
8. 80÷4
10. 4x8
12. 314-10
13. 20-2
14. 410+7
16. 5x5
18. Six hundred and four.

Down

1. 12x12
2. A dozen
3. Six thousand
5. 60-8
7. Nine hundred and thirty
9. 100+38
11. 18+6
12. 3x11
13. 12+5
15. 140-4
16. 7x3
17. 8+6

The answer to this puzzle is on page 226.

Cool Crossnumbers

puzzle 72

Across

1. Seven hundred and two
3. 150+16
5. 5000+5
7. 40÷4
8. 33x10
9. 900-25
11. 8x9
13. 49x10
14. 120-11
15. Nine thousand and twenty-three

Down

1. 700+25
2. Two hundred and sixty
3. Unlucky number!
4. 8x80
6. 60-7
7. One thousand and seventy-nine
10. 500+49
12. 4x5
13. 800÷2
14. 27-10

The answer to this puzzle
is on page 226.

Cool Crossnumbers

puzzle 73

Across
1. Seven thousand, four hundred and fifteen
3. 4x8
4. 50x10
5. 144÷12
6. 9x9
8. 700+86
11. 300-20
13. 12x12
14. Eight hundred
16. 74-5
17. 49-7

Down
1. 11x7
2. 562-10
3. Three hundred and eight
5. 21-5
7. One thousand
9. Eighty-three
10. 110+14
12. 6x3
13. 99+7
15. 2x12

The answer to this puzzle is on page 226.

Cool Crossnumbers

puzzle 74

The grid as filled in:

Row 1: 1 8, 2 7 3
Row 2: 3 6 0, 0
Row 3: 3 1, 6 1 6
Row 4: 7, 1 0 2
Row 5: 9 0 0 0, 2
Row 6: 1 0 2 4
Row 7: 3 1 1, 4
Row 8: 5, 1 8 0 2

Across
1. Eighteen
3. 300−25
5. 10x50
6. 26+4
7. 609+7
8. 108−6
9. 1000x9
11. 999+25
13. 360+11
15. One thousand, eight hundred and two

Down
2. 799+51
3. 60÷3
4. Five thousand and twelve
6. Three hundred and seventy-nine
7. 10x6
8. 96+5
10. 2x12
12. 250−8
13. 7x5
14. 22÷2

The answer to this puzzle is on page 227.

Cool Crossnumbers

puzzle 75

Across

1. 6x9
2. Three thousand, three hundred and thirty -three
4. Two dozen
5. 610+30
7. 500÷5
9. 4x4
10. 8x11
13. 571-2
14. 500+ 500
15. 100-3
16. 5x5

Down

1. 500+16
2. 42-8
3. 3x1000
4. 100÷5
6. 460+16
8. 4x7
9. 26÷2
11. 900-50
12. Eight thousand, nine hundred and fifteen
14. 13+4

The answer to this puzzle is on page 227.

Cool Crossnumbers

puzzle 76

Across
1. 176-13
3. 345+421
5. 503+4
6. Forty-one thousand
8. 15+8
9. 6x14
11. 51+76
13. 732-48

Down
1. 1001+23
2. 7x5
3. Seven thousand, seven hundred and ninety
4. 10x60
7. 12x12
8. Two hundred and forty-seven
9. 423x2
10. 66÷6
12. 8x3

The answer to this puzzle is on page 227.

Cool Crossnumbers

puzzle 77

Across

1. Four thousand, two hundred and fifty-six
3. 9x6
4. 7x7
6. Two thousand, nine hundred and sixty-seven
9. 400÷10
10. Three dozen
11. 692+70
14. 20-7
17. 100-36
18. 7000+625

Down

2. 40-12
3. 118÷2
4. 29+18
5. 740-17
7. 200-104
8. 11x7
9. 7x6
12. 680÷10
13. 150-64
15. 15+22
16. 9x5

The answer to this puzzle is on page 228.

Cool Crossnumbers

puzzle 78

Across

1. Four hundred and sixty-two
5. 549+15
6. 44÷2
7. 67+29
9. 7600÷100
10. 9x6
13. 500-275
16. 30÷2
17. 700-17
18. 180x2

Down

1. 4x12
2. 260-3
3. 50-26
4. Eight thousand, nine hundred and twenty-six
6. 22+5
8. 100-35
11. 273+4000
12. 5x5
14. 1000-250
15. 18x2
16. 9+7

> The answer to this puzzle is on page 228.

Cool Crossnumbers

puzzle 79

Across
1. 560+19
3. 31+48
5. 12+5
7. 28×3
9. 6×6
10. 77−4
12. 100−8
13. 6000+549
15. 24÷2
17. 40+8
18. 500−255

Down
1. 70−13
2. 100−9
4. Nine thousand, two hundred and forty-six
6. 90−12
8. One thousand, seven hundred and sixty-seven
11. 27+8
12. 150−51
14. 102×4
15. 144÷12
16. 48÷2

The answer to this puzzle is on page 228.

Cool Crossnumbers

puzzle 80

Across
1. 50×7
3. 30−13
5. 35+31
6. 50−23
7. 110×2
10. Five thousand, four hundred and thirty-two
11. 11×11
13. 21+12
14. 100−11
16. 32×3
17. 610+101

Down
1. Three thousand, six hundred and seventy-two
2. 41+15
4. 3×25
6. 100÷5
8. 444÷2
9. 106+38
12. 150−14
14. 9×9
15. 120−29

The answer to this puzzle is on page 228.

Hardcore Hanjie

How To Do Hanjie

The brilliant thing about Hanjie is that when you've completed a puzzle you not only get a huge amount of satisfaction, but also a picture.

A Hanjie puzzle consists of a grid of empty white squares. To the right of each row and beneath each column you will find a clue of one or more numbers.

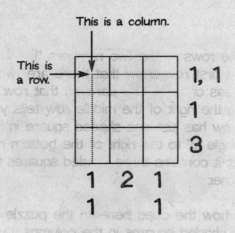

This is a column.

This is a row.

1, 1

1

3

1 2 1
1   1

To see the picture develop all you have to do is follow the clues and fill in the correct squares in the grid — it's kind of like being a cross between Einstein and Picasso!

The clues tell you how many squares you should shade in on each line. The tricky part is working out where on the line they go.

A simple example of a finished puzzle looks like this:

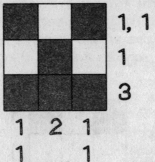

See how the clue numbers match the number of shaded squares?

Look at the rows — the two numbers '1, 1' to the right of the first row show that there are two shaded areas of length 1 square on that row. The single '1' to the right of the middle row tells you that that row has just one shaded square in it, and the single '3' to the right of the bottom row shows that it contains three shaded squares next to each other.

Now look how the clues beneath the puzzle match the shaded squares in the columns.

Getting Started

To solve a Hanjie puzzle all you need to do is shade in the correct number of squares in each row and column. However, the clues tell you only how many squares to shade in — it's up to you to work out where they are.

Look at the top row of the example below. The clue tells us that it needs to contain two areas of length '1'. They can't touch because if they did, it would be just one area of length 2. So to fit both into the three squares available, they have to go like this:

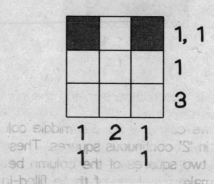

The bottom row is similar — there is only one place the '3' filled squares will fit:

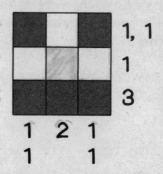

The middle row can't be solved yet because there are three possible places that the single filled square could fit.

Let's have a look at the columns to help figure it out:

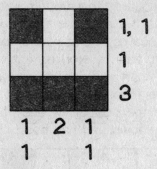

The left column and the right column are already solved, so we can now try the middle column. We have to fill in '2' continuous squares. These can't be the top two squares of the column because this would make a column of three filled-in squares, not two, (and would make the top row wrong). So, the solution must be:

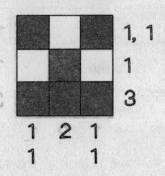

Easy, isn't it? Here are some extra tricks to help you tackle the puzzles and become a hardcore Hanjie-er!

Tackling Trick One

Mark any squares that you know are empty with a tiny cross. If the clue is '0' you know there are NO filled squares in that row or column. You can often get further by working out which squares are empty than you can by working out which squares are filled! Have a look at this example row, where the position of one of the three squares is known and has been filled in:

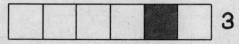

The three filled squares will fit in only two different positions — the shaded one and the squares on either side of it, or the shaded one and the two squares to the left of it. Both of these solutions leave the two squares on the far left empty, so you can mark them with a cross.

Tackling Trick Two

It is also helpful to mark in squares that *must* be filled, even if you don't yet know the whole solution to a clue.

For example, have a look at this row of five squares:

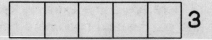

The furthest left the '3' filled squares will fit is:

and the furthest right the squares will fit is:

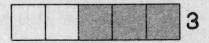

Can you see that the middle square is filled in however the block of '3' is placed? That means you can officially shade it in:

It's always worth giving this tackling trick a go if the clue number is equal to or greater than half the total number of squares in the column or row.

Top Tips

• The puzzles get harder as you work through the chapter, so start at the beginning.

• No guessing. All the puzzles can be solved by following the clues and figuring out which squares should be shaded.

• There is only one possible solution for each puzzle, so if your picture doesn't look like the answer in the back of the book, you've gone wrong somewhere.

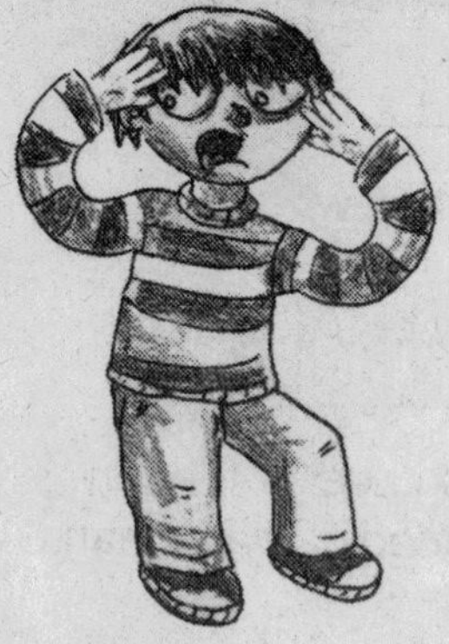

Hardcore Hanjie

puzzle 81
Upstairs

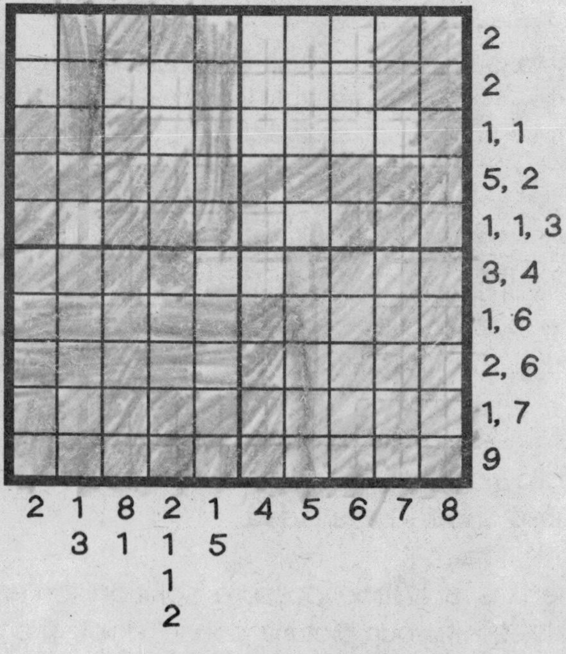
2
2
1, 1
5, 2
1, 1, 3
3, 4
1, 6
2, 6
1, 7
9
2
1 3
8 1
2 1 1 2
1 5
4
5
6
7
8

The answer to this puzzle is on page 229.

Hardcore Hanjie

puzzle 82
Sail Away

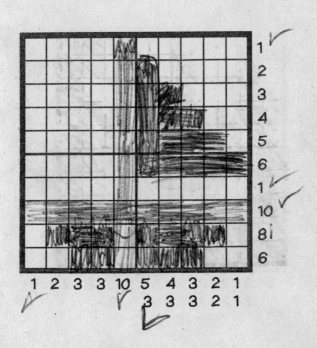

The answer to this puzzle
is on page 229.

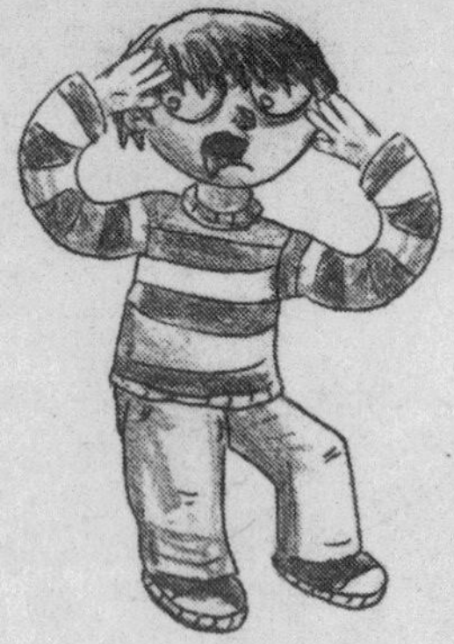

Hardcore Hanjie

puzzle 83
Time

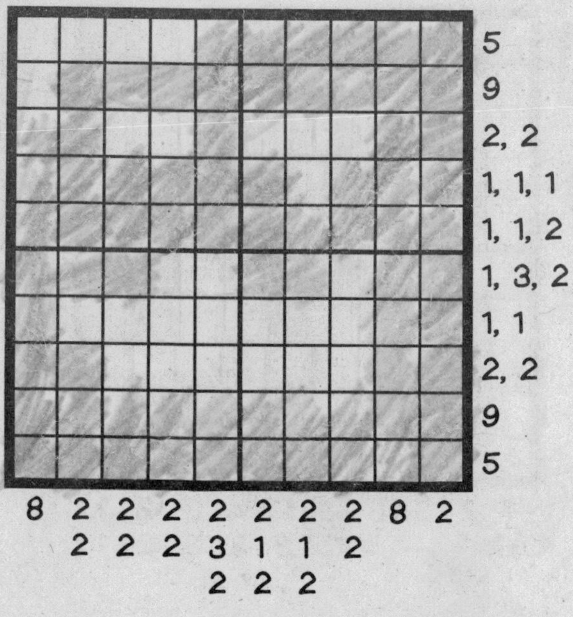
5
9
2, 2
1, 1, 1
1, 1, 2
1, 3, 2
1, 1
2, 2
9
5
8
2 2
2 2
2 2
2 3 2
2 1 2
2 1 2
2 2
8
2

The answer to this puzzle is on page 230.

Hardcore Hanjie

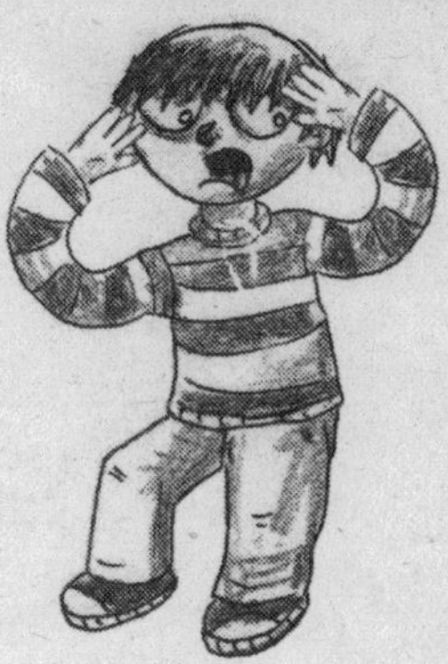

puzzle 84
Spray

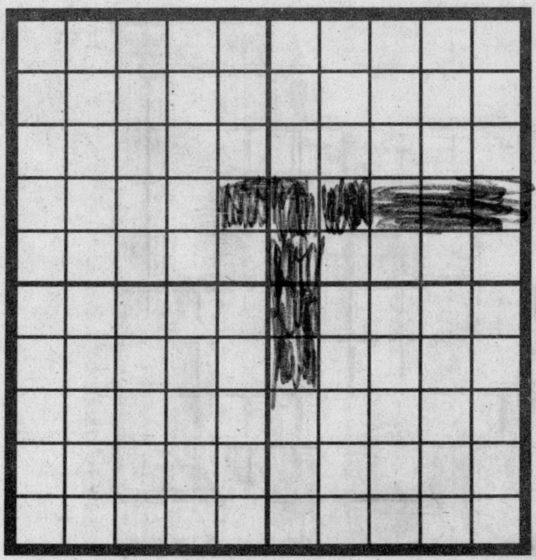

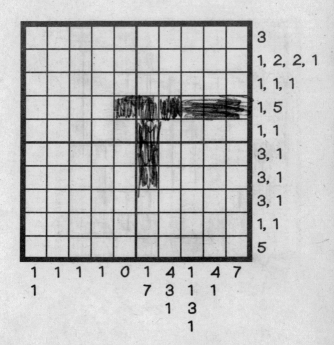

Row clues:
3
1, 2, 2, 1
1, 1, 1
1, 5
1, 1
3, 1
3, 1
3, 1
1, 1
5

Column clues:
1 1
1
1
1
0
1 7
4 3 1
1 1 3 1
4 1
7

The answer to this puzzle is on page 230.

Hardcore Hanjie

puzzle 85
Pants

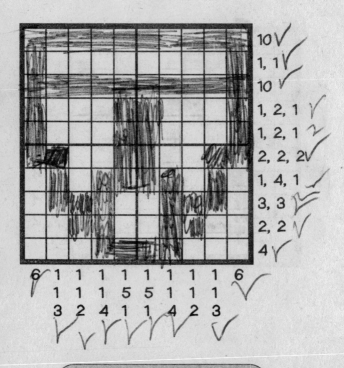

Row clues:

10
1, 1
10
1, 2, 1
1, 2, 1
2, 2, 2
1, 4, 1
3, 3
2, 2
4

Column clues:

6	1	1	1	1	1	1	1	1	6
	1	1	1	5	5	1	1	1	
	3	2	4	1	1	4	2	3	

The answer to this puzzle is on page 231.

Hardcore Hanjie

puzzle 86
Musical

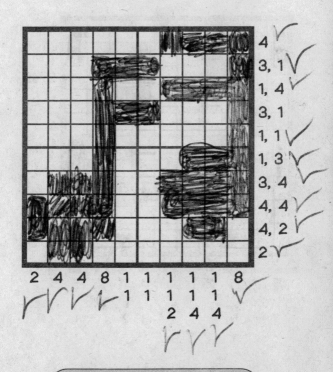

The answer to this puzzle is on page 231.

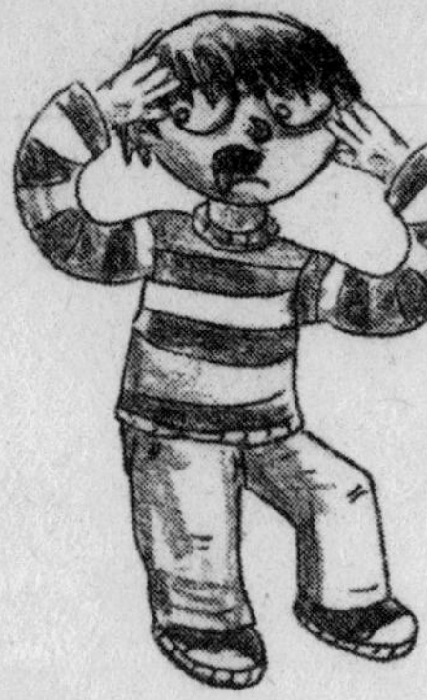

Hardcore Hanjie

puzzle 87
Wink

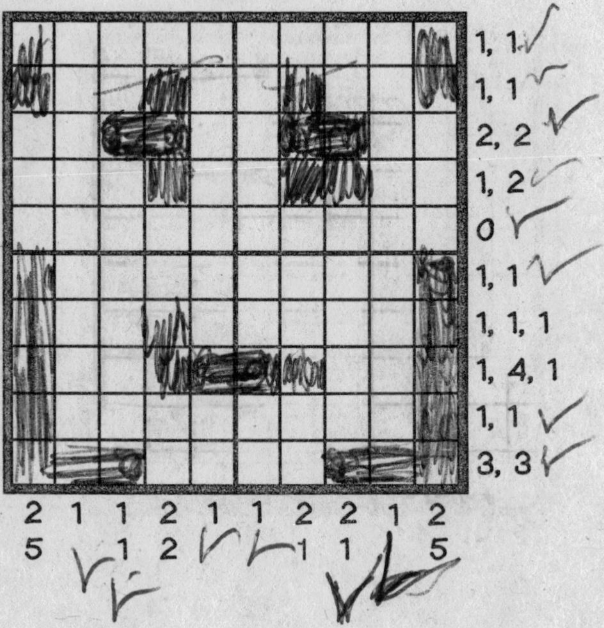
1, 1
1, 1
2, 2
1, 2
0
1, 1
1, 1, 1
1, 4, 1
1, 1
3, 3
2 5
1
1 1
2 2
1
1
2 1
2 1
1
2 5

The answer to this puzzle is on page 232.

Hardcore Hanjie

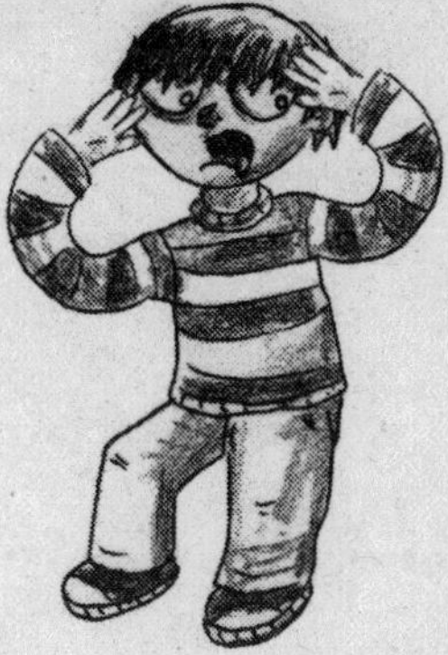

puzzle 88
Leafy

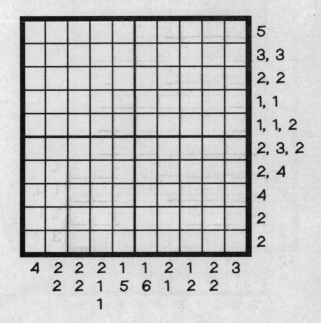

Row clues (right of grid):

5
3, 3
2, 2
1, 1
1, 1, 2
2, 3, 2
2, 4
4
2
2

Column clues (below grid):

4 | 2 2 | 2 2 | 2 1 1 | 1 5 | 1 6 | 2 1 | 1 2 | 2 2 | 3

The answer to this puzzle is on page 232.

Hardcore Hanjie

puzzle 89
Sit!

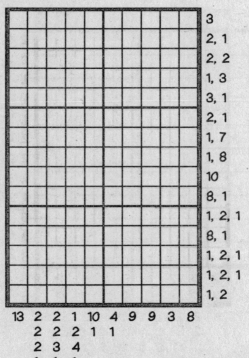

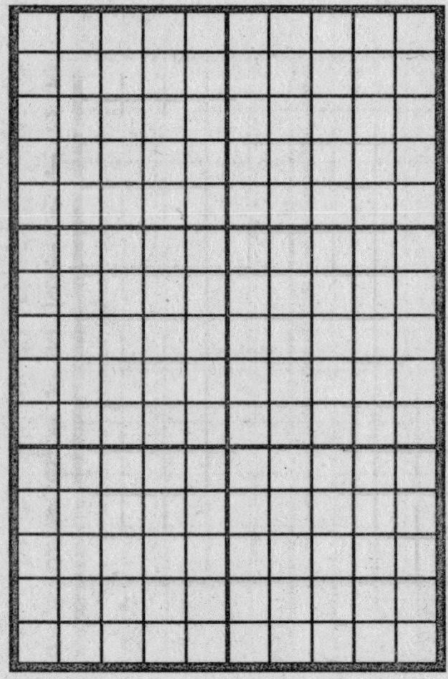
3
2, 1
2, 2
1, 3
3, 1
2, 1
1, 7
1, 8
10
8, 1
1, 2, 1
8, 1
1, 2, 1
1, 2, 1
1, 2
13
2 2 2 1
2 2 3 1
1 2 4 1
10 1
4 1
9
9
3
8

The answer to this puzzle is on page 233.

Hardcore Hanjie

puzzle 90
Electric

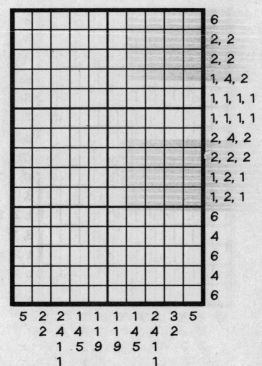

Row clues (top to bottom):
6
2, 2
2, 2
1, 4, 2
1, 1, 1, 1
1, 1, 1, 1
2, 4, 2
2, 2, 2
1, 2, 1
1, 2, 1
6
4
6
4
6

Column clues (left to right):

5	2	2	1	1	1	1	2	3	5
2	4	4	1	1	4	4	2		
1	5	9	9	5	1				
1					1				

The answer to this puzzle is on page 233.

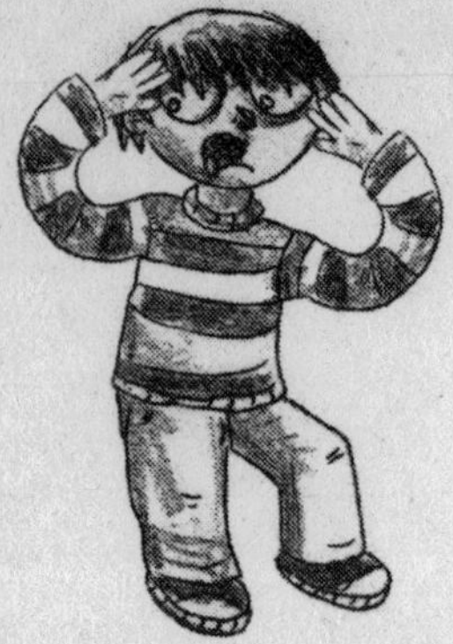

Hardcore Hanjie

puzzle 91
Icebird

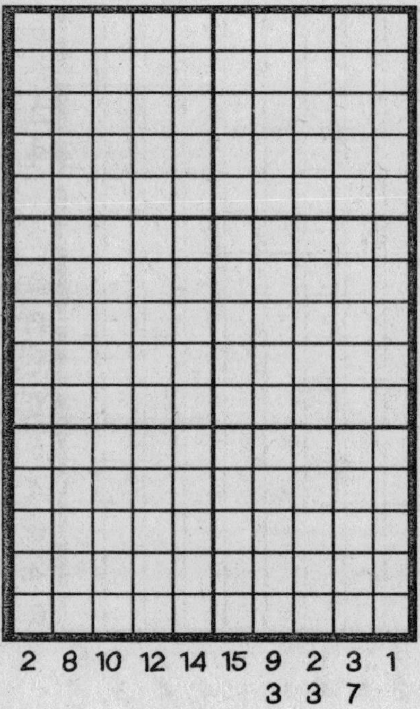

Row clues:

3
5
4, 2
6
5
7
5, 1
6, 1
6, 1
5, 1
5, 1
5, 2
7
7
3, 4

Column clues:

2 | 8 | 10 | 12 | 14 | 15 | 9 3 | 2 3 2 1 | 3 7 | 1

The answer to this puzzle is on page 234.

Hardcore Hanjie

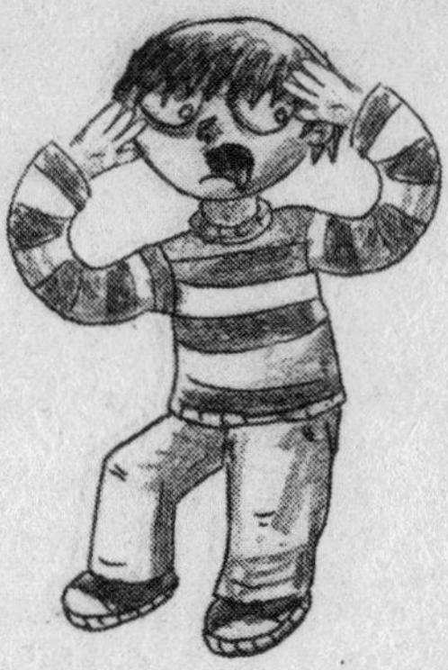

puzzle 92
Cone

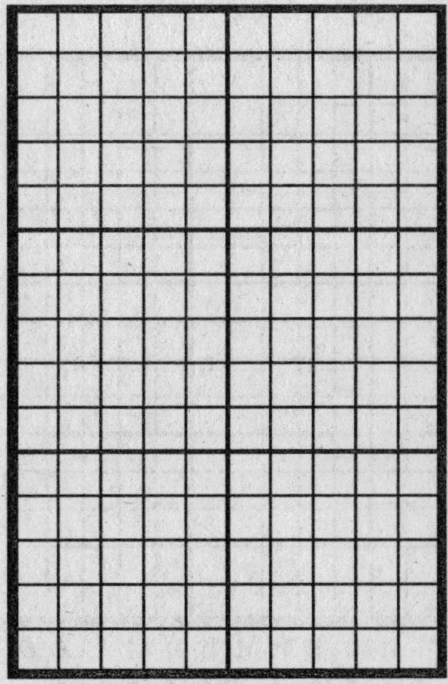

Row clues (top to bottom): 3, 1 / 2, 2, 2 / 1, 4 / 1, 2 / 1, 1 / 1, 1 / 10 / 10 / 9 / 8 / 6 / 6 / 4 / 4 / 2

Column clues (left to right): 4 / 2 4 / 2 6 / 2 8 / 1 9 / 2 9 / 2 8 / 2 6 / 4 4 / 3 3

The answer to this puzzle is on page 234.

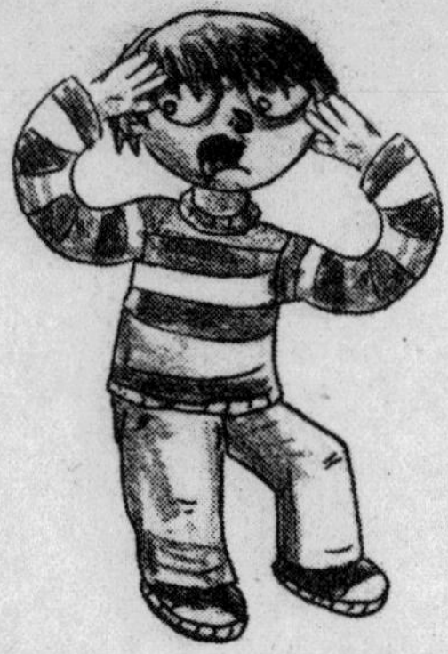

Hardcore Hanjie

puzzle 93
Cuppa

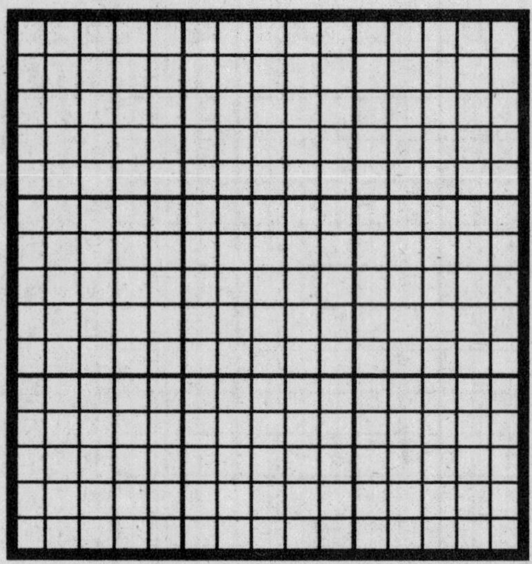

Row clues (top to bottom):
- 0
- 11
- 13
- 11, 2
- 11, 1
- 11, 1
- 11, 1
- 11, 1
- 11, 2
- 13
- 11
- 9
- 0
- 14
- 12

Column clues (left to right):
- 1
- 10 2
- 11 2
- 11 2
- 11 2
- 11 2
- 11 2
- 11 2
- 11 2
- 11 2
- 11 2
- 10 2
- 1 1 2
- 2 2 1
- 6

The answer to this puzzle is on page 235.

Hardcore Hanjie

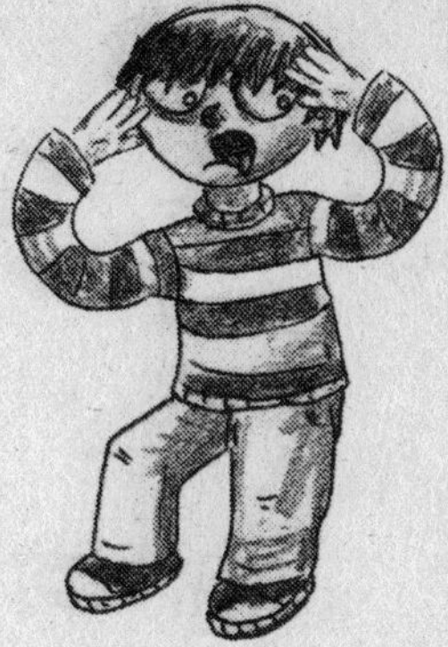

puzzle 94
Granny Smith

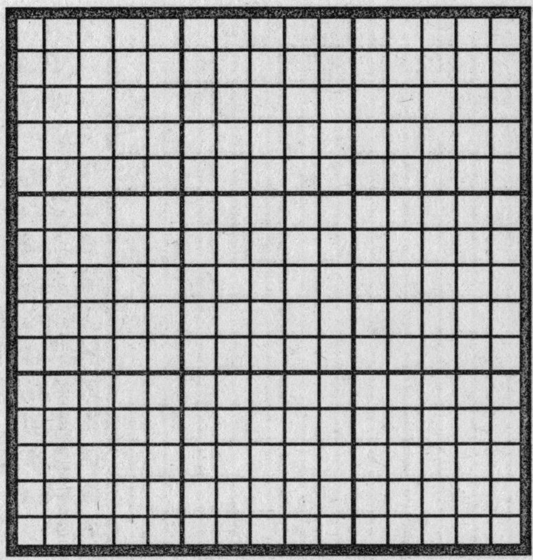

Row clues (top to bottom):
3
3
5, 1
3, 4, 4
3, 11
2, 11
2, 11
2, 11
2, 10
3, 10
4, 9
4, 8
11
9
7

Column clues (left to right):
7
9
3 4
2 4
1 4 4
8 3
13
12
14
2 11
2 12
1 11
10
9
7

The answer to this puzzle is on page 235.

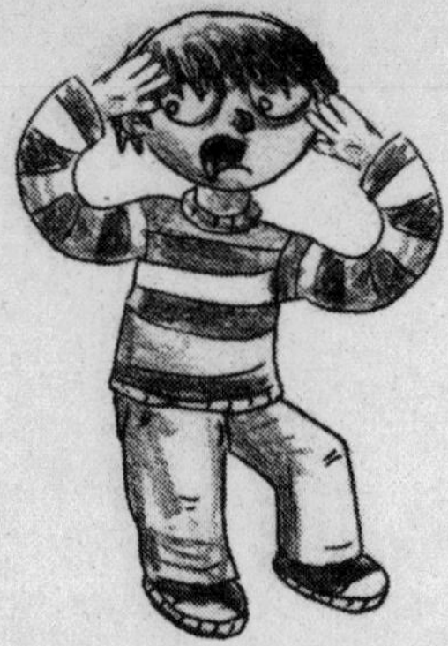

Hardcore Hanjie

puzzle 95
Scary

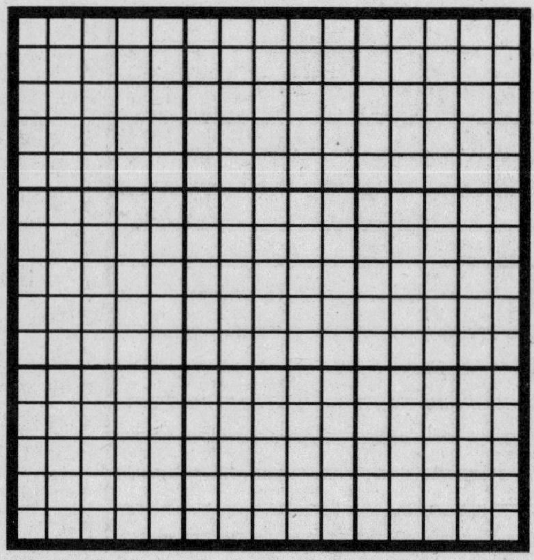

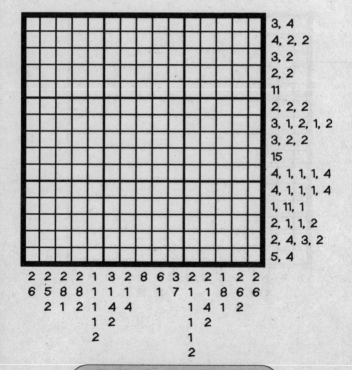

Row clues:

3, 4
4, 2, 2
3, 2
2, 2
11
2, 2, 2
3, 1, 2, 1, 2
3, 2, 2
15
4, 1, 1, 1, 4
4, 1, 1, 1, 4
1, 11, 1
2, 1, 1, 2
2, 4, 3, 2
5, 4

Column clues:

2	2	2	2	1	3	2	8	6	3	2	2	1	2	2
6	5	8	8	1	1	1		1	7	1	1	8	6	6
	2	1	2	1	4	4				1	4	1	2	
				1	2					1	2			
				2						1				
										2				

The answer to this puzzle is on page 236.

Hardcore Hanjie

puzzle 96
Faithful

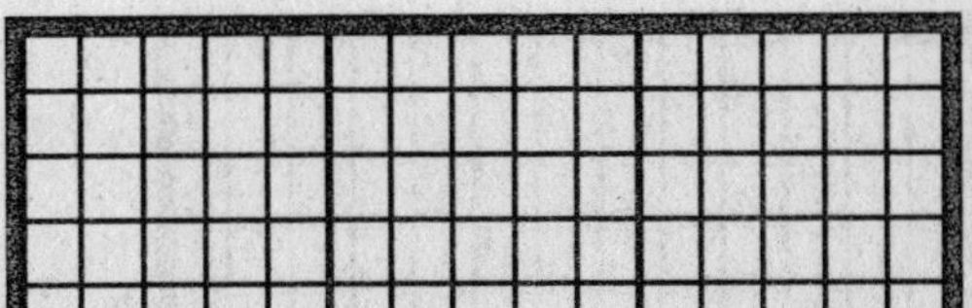

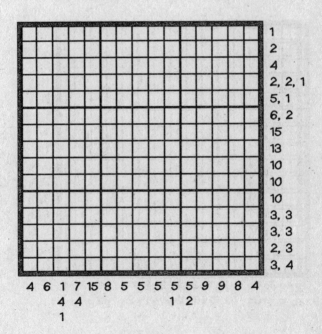

Row clues (top to bottom): 1 / 2 / 4 / 2, 2, 1 / 5, 1 / 6, 2 / 15 / 13 / 10 / 10 / 10 / 3, 3 / 3, 3 / 2, 3 / 3, 4

Column clues (left to right): 4 / 6 / 1 4 1 / 7 4 / 15 / 8 / 5 / 5 / 5 / 5 1 / 5 2 / 9 / 9 / 8 / 4

The answer to this puzzle is on page 236.

Hardcore Hanjie

puzzle 97
Aweigh!

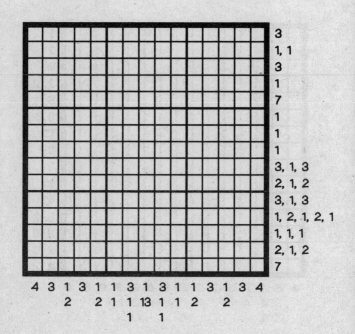

Row clues (top to bottom):
3
1, 1
3
1
7
1
1
1
3, 1, 3
2, 1, 2
3, 1, 3
1, 2, 1, 2, 1
1, 1, 1
2, 1, 2
7

Column clues (left to right):
4 3 1 3 1 1 3 1 3 1 1 3 1 3 4
2   2 1 1 1 1 1 1 2   2
          1   1

The answer to this puzzle
is on page 237.

Hardcore Hanjie

puzzle 98
Red and Ripe

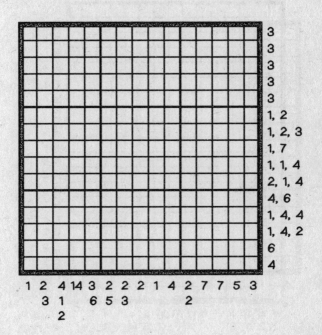

Row clues (top to bottom):

3
3
3
3
3
1, 2
1, 2, 3
1, 7
1, 1, 4
2, 1, 4
4, 6
1, 4, 4
1, 4, 2
6
4

Column clues (left to right):

1	2	4	14	3	2	2	2	1	4	2	7	7	5	3
	3	1		6	5	3				2				
		2												

The answer to this puzzle is on page 237.

Hardcore Hanjie

puzzle 99
Senior citizen

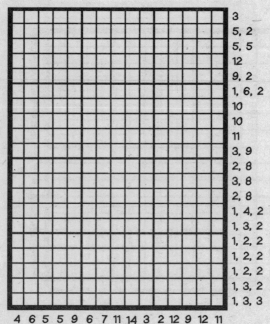

Row clues (top to bottom):
3
5, 2
5, 5
12
9, 2
1, 6, 2
10
10
11
3, 9
2, 8
3, 8
2, 8
1, 4, 2
1, 3, 2
1, 2, 2
1, 2, 2
1, 2, 2
1, 3, 2
1, 3, 3

Column clues (left to right):
4 6 5 5 9 6 7 11 14 3 2 12 9 12 11
   2 11 6   2 15 14 1

The answer to this puzzle
is on page 238.

Hardcore Hanjie

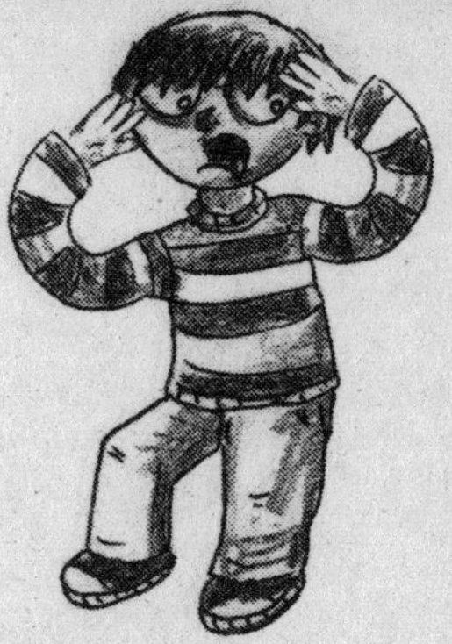

puzzle 100
Traffic

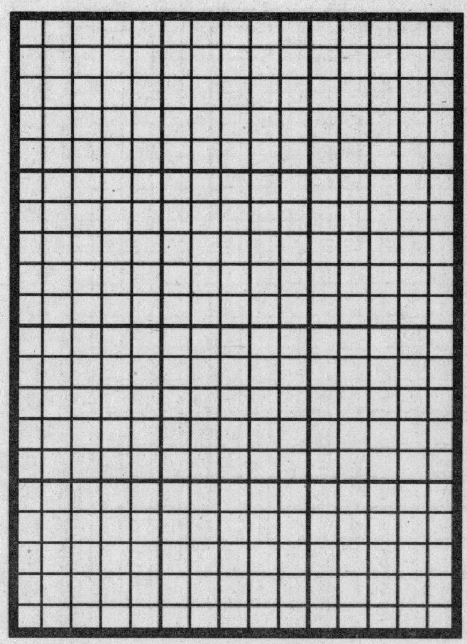

Row clues:

4
5
0
6
1, 3, 2
6, 3
5, 3
2, 4, 2
2, 2, 2
1, 9, 2
10, 2
4, 4, 4
2, 3, 5
2, 3, 2
1, 4
5
7
7
0
7

Column clues:

6
2 3
2
3
1 2
1 3 6 2 1
2 1 3 5 2 1
2 5 4 3 1
2 9 4 1
2 8 5 1
2 1 6 1
1 7 1
2 2
10
10

The answer to this puzzle is on page 238.

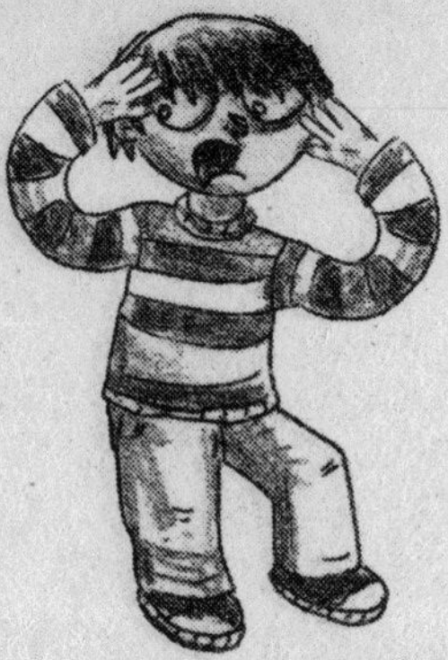

Hardcore Hanjie

puzzle 101
Prickly

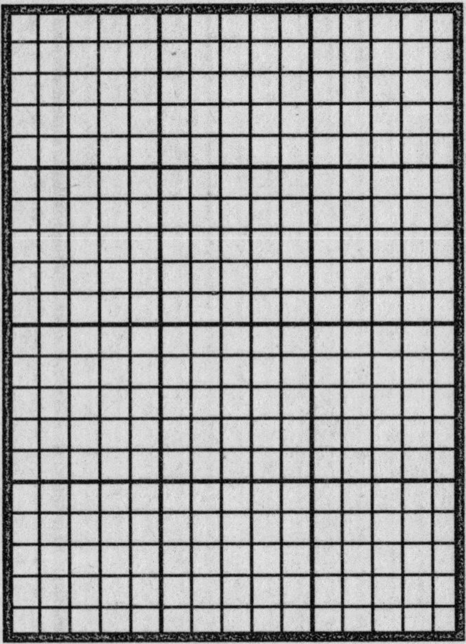

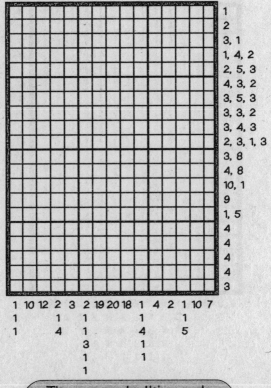

Row clues (top to bottom):

1
2
3, 1
1, 4, 2
2, 5, 3
4, 3, 2
3, 5, 3
3, 3, 2
3, 4, 3
2, 3, 1, 3
3, 8
4, 8
10, 1
9
1, 5
4
4
4
4
3

Column clues (left to right):

1	10	12	2	3	2	19	20	18	1	4	2	1	10	7
1			1		1				1			1		
1			4		1				4			5		
					3				1					
					1				1					
					1									

The answer to this puzzle is on page 239.

Hardcore Hanjie

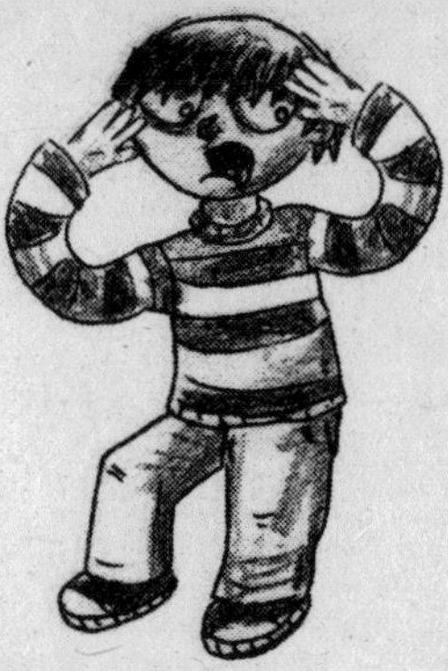

puzzle 102
Pink

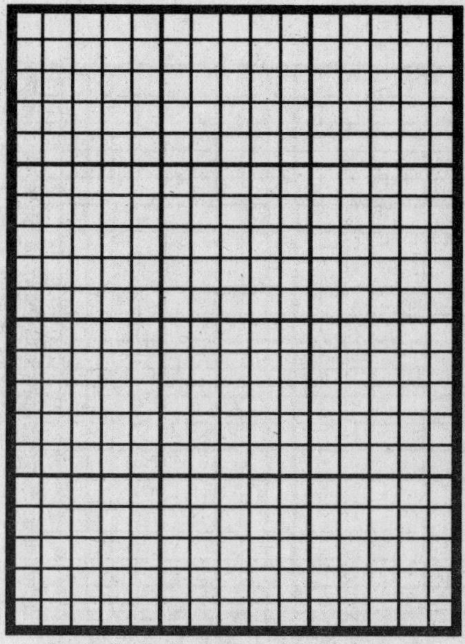

Row clues (top to bottom): 4 | 3, 2 | 6 | 2 | 3 | 2 | 3 | 4, 2 | 10 | 11 | 12 | 9 | 6 | 1, 1 | 2, 1 | 6 | 1, 1 | 1 | 1 | 3

Column clues (left to right): 1 | 3 | 4 | 5 | 6 2 | 9 | 6 1 | 13 | 3 5 1 1 | 6 4 2 1 | 3 7 | 3 5 | 1 1 | 3 | 1

The answer to this puzzle is on page 239.

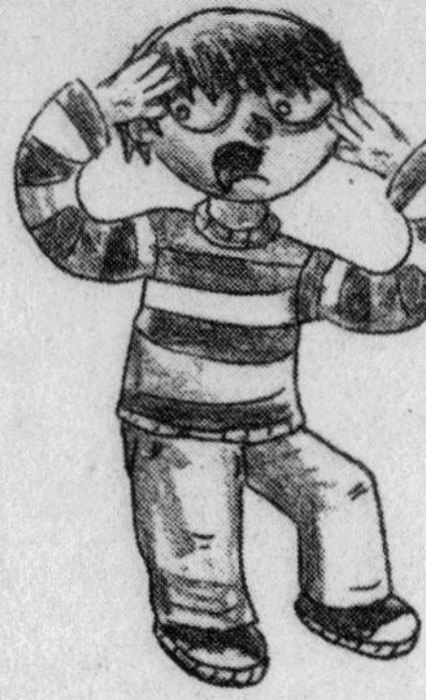

Hardcore Hanjie

puzzle 103
Trunk

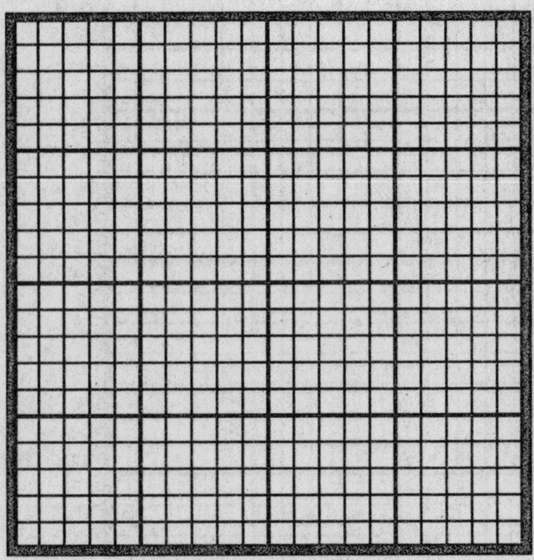

Row clues (top to bottom):
2
4
6
7
8
15
3, 14
20
20
20
20
2, 1, 14
2, 2, 14
1, 14
1, 13
1, 5, 3, 1
1, 3, 3, 1
3, 3, 3
3, 3
4, 4

Column clues (left to right):
11
7 1
6 1
7 1
4 6
10
14
16 1
19
18
17
11
10
10
10 1
15
15
14
9
10

The answer to this puzzle is on page 240.

Hardcore Hanjie

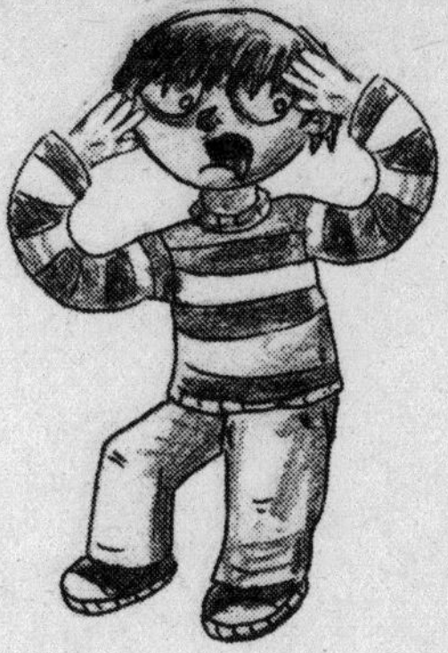

puzzle 104
Airborne

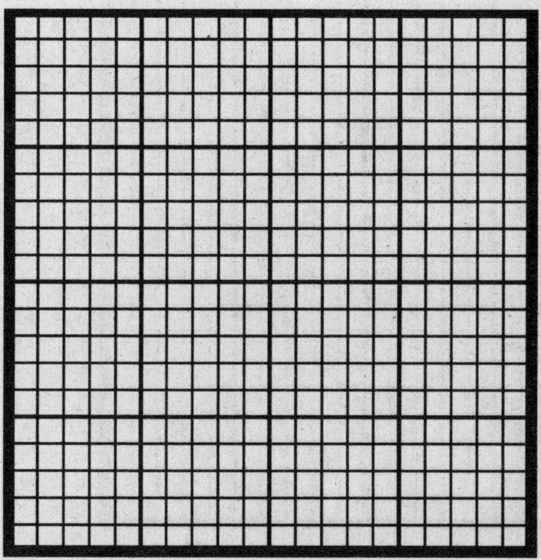

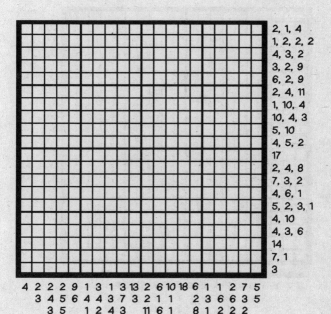

Row clues (top to bottom):

2, 1, 4
1, 2, 2, 2
4, 3, 2
3, 2, 9
6, 2, 9
2, 4, 11
1, 10, 4
10, 4, 3
5, 10
4, 5, 2
17
2, 4, 8
7, 3, 2
4, 6, 1
5, 2, 3, 1
4, 10
4, 3, 6
14
7, 1
3

Column clues (left to right):

4
2 3
2 4 3
2 5 5
9 6
1 4 1 7
3 4 2 3 3
1 3 4 3
3 7 3
13 3
2 2 11
6 1 6
10 1 1 1
18
6 2 8
1 3 1 3 4
1 6 2 3
2 6 2 2
7 3 2
5 5

The answer to this puzzle is on page 240.

Hardcore Hanjie

puzzle 105
Bedtime

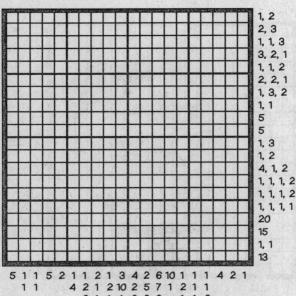

The answer to this puzzle
is on page 240.

Tai-Chi
Towers

Tai-Chi Towers

Have you got what it takes to tackle a Tai-Chi Tower? Can you progress all the way from a white-belt beginner to a black-belt boss?

Every number in a box is the sum of the two numbers in the boxes beneath it added together. Fill in each empty box with the correct number to complete the tower.

Top Tip: There are two ways of figuring out the missing numbers. You can either add the two numbers below the empty box together or subtract the number beside the empty box from the number they share above.

puzzle 106

Look how these two numbers added together equal the number in the box above.

The answer to this puzzle is on page 241.

Tai-Chi Towers

puzzle 107

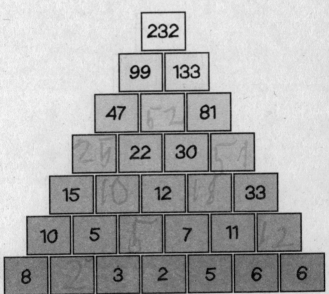

```
                    232
                 99     133
              47      52    81
           29    22     30    51
        15    10    12    18    33
     10     5    5     7    11    12
   8    2    3    2    5    6    6
```

The answer to this puzzle
is on page 241.

Tai-Chi
Towers

puzzle 108

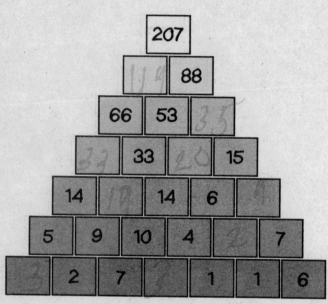

	207	
	88	
66	53	
33		15
14	14	6
5	9	10	4	7
2	7	1	1	6

The answer to this puzzle
is on page 242.

Tai-Chi Towers

puzzle 109

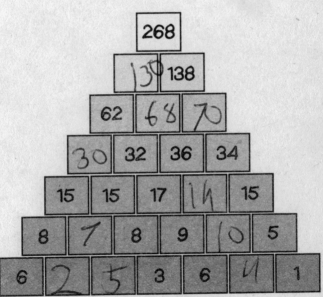

	268	

| 130 | 138 |

| 62 | 68 | 70 |

| 30 | 32 | 36 | 34 |

| 15 | 15 | 17 | 14 | 15 |

| 8 | 7 | 8 | 9 | 10 | 5 |

| 6 | 2 | 5 | 3 | 6 | 4 | 1 |

The answer to this puzzle
is on page 242.

Tai-Chi Towers

puzzle 110

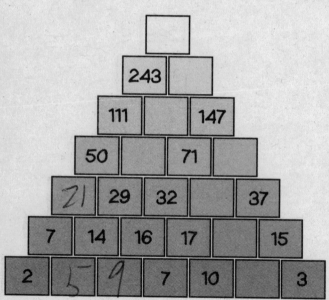

The answer to this puzzle is on page 243.

Tai-Chi Towers

puzzle 111

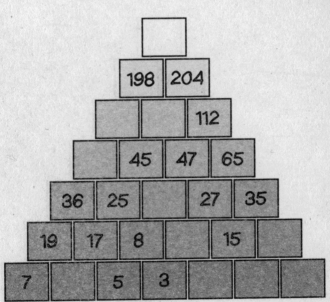

The answer to this puzzle is on page 243.

Tai-Chi Towers

puzzle 112

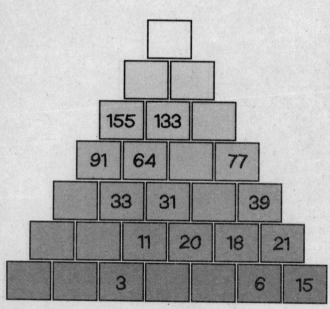

The answer to this puzzle
is on page 244.

Tai-Chi Towers

puzzle 113

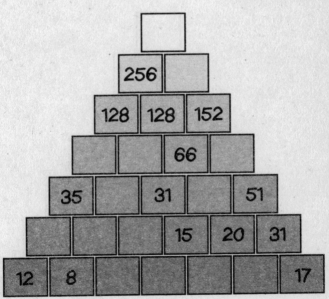

The answer to this puzzle is on page 244.

Tai-Chi Towers

puzzle 114

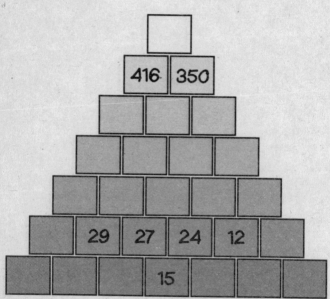

The answer to this puzzle
is on page 245.

Tai-Chi
Towers

puzzle 115

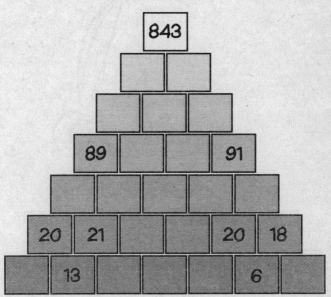

The answer to this puzzle
is on page 245.

Battleships
Bonanza

How To Play Battleships

Ever wondered how good your naval navigation skills are? Well now you can find out, with these Battleship puzzles!

To solve a Battleship puzzle you have to follow number clues which allow you to locate and destroy enemy ships.

A Battleship puzzle consists of a grid of empty squares in which a selection of different ships are hidden. Your task is to work out which squares are just empty water, and which contain part of a battleship.

Fleet Details

On the left of the grid is a list that tells you how many ships make up the enemy fleet hidden in the grid and how large they are. These are the ships you will come across:

Submarines are 1 square long.

Destroyers are 2 squares long.

Cruisers are 3 squares long.

Battleships are 4 squares long.

Aircraft carriers are 5 squares long.

There are two important rules that you need to remember about ships:

1. Ships are always arranged in a horizontal or vertical straight line — they are never diagonal or any other shape.

2. Ships NEVER, EVER, touch each other horizontally or vertically, but they CAN touch diagonally.

The Grid

Beside each row and below each column in the grid you will find a number. This number tells you how many squares in that row or column are filled with parts of a ship. What it doesn't tell you is exactly which squares they are.

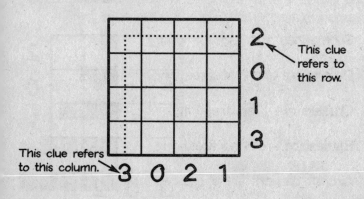

Getting Started

Here is a typical battleship puzzle:

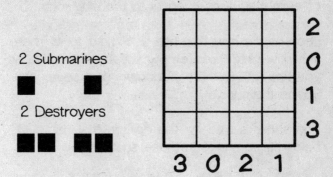

2 Submarines

2 Destroyers

From the list of ships hidden in the puzzle, you can see that you need to find two submarines, which are 1 square long, and two destroyers, which are 2 squares long.

Tackling Trick One

All the squares in rows or columns marked with a '0' have no ship segments in them. Mark these as empty water by placing a tiny cross in them:

2 Submarines

2 Destroyers

Tackling Trick Two

Check for rows and columns where the number of empty squares is equal to the clue total.

Look at the row that has a '3' next to it. There are now only three empty squares left on it, so you know they must all contain ship segments. Shade them in.

The same is true for the column that has a '3' below it, so shade in these squares too.

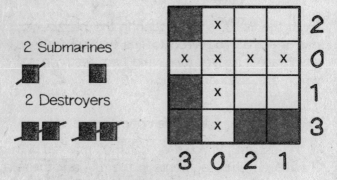

2 Submarines

2 Destroyers

Now look at the shaded squares. You have located both destroyers and one of the submarines, so you can cross them out on the fleet details. Just one submarine left to find!

Tackling Trick Three

You know that ships never touch, so put a cross in the squares next to the ships you've found. For example, you can mark the squares above the destroyer at the bottom-right of the grid with a cross.

158

It is useful to realize that you could also have worked this out by looking at which rows and columns already contain the correct number of ship segments. For example, look at the row with the '1' next to it. There is already one square filled in, so the rest of the squares must contain water. The same is true for the column with the '1' below it. This means you can mark the square at the top right with a cross too.

2 Submarines

2 Destroyers

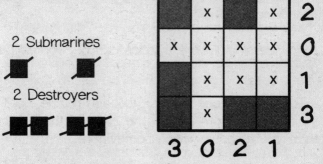

Almost Done

There is now just one empty square left, so that must be where the submarine is located. Shade it in.

2 Submarines

2 Destroyers

That's it — all enemy ships have been successfully located and destroyed. Mission accomplished.

159

Top Tips

• The puzzles get steadily harder as you work through the chapter, so start at the beginning.

• Always start by marking all the squares where the clue for the row or column is '0' as water.

• Look at the rows and columns with the highest number of ship segments in them, and see if you can place any.

• Work back and forth between trying to place water and trying to place ship segments until you've either solved the puzzle or gotten stuck.

• When you have filled in two or more squares of a ship don't forget to mark all the squares alongside it as water. You can do this even if you don't yet know exactly how long the ship is.

• If you get stuck, try working out where you can fit the largest ship.

• No guessing! All the puzzles can be worked out using logic.

• There's only one solution to each puzzle, so if yours differs from that at the back of the book then you've gone wrong somewhere.

Battleship Bonanza

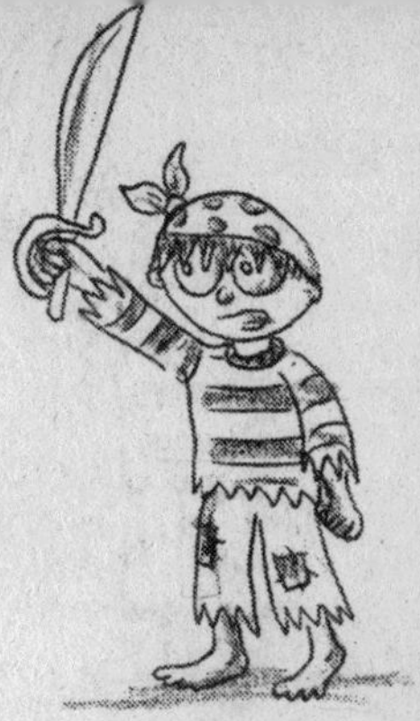

puzzle 116

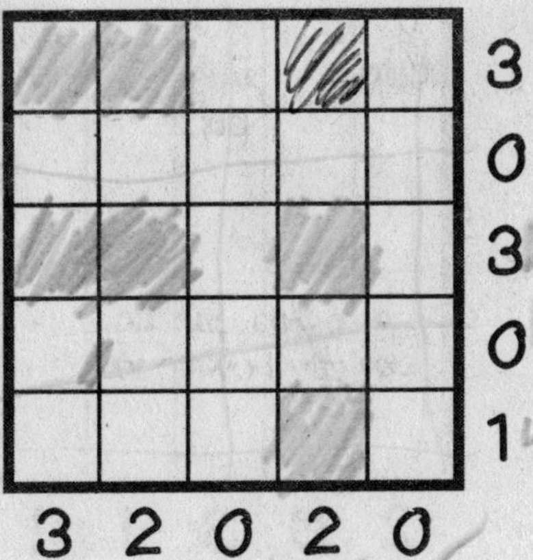

3 Submarines

2 Destroyers

The answer to this puzzle is on page 246.

Battleship Bonanza

puzzle 117

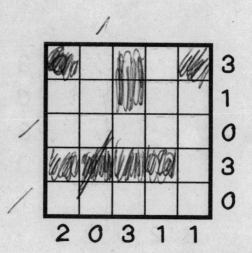

3
1
0
3
0

2 0 3 1 1

3 Submarines   2 Destroyers

The answer to this puzzle
is on page 246.

Battleship
Bonanza

puzzle 118

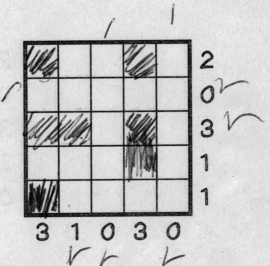

3 Submarines   2 Destroyers

The answer to this puzzle
is on page 246.

Battleship Bonanza

puzzle 119

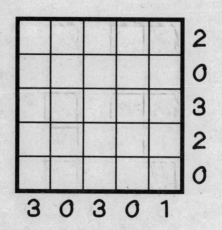

Columns (left to right): 3 0 3 0 1
Rows (top to bottom): 2 0 3 2 0

3 Submarines

2 Destroyers

The answer to this puzzle is on page 246.

Battleship Bonanza

puzzle 120

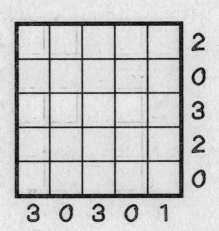

Row clues (top to bottom): 2, 0, 3, 2, 0

Column clues (left to right): 3, 0, 3, 0, 1

3 Submarines

2 Destroyers

The answer to this puzzle
is on page 247.

Battleship Bonanza

puzzle 121

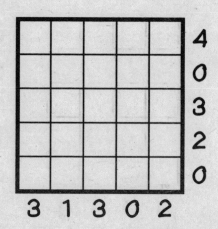

					4
-----	-----	-----	-----	-----	0
					3
					2
					0

3 1 3 0 2

2 Submarines

2 Destroyers

1 Cruiser

The answer to this puzzle
is on page 247.

Battleship
Bonanza

puzzle 122

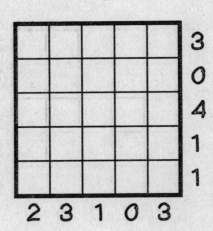

3
0
4
1
1

2 3 1 0 3

2 Submarines

2 Destroyers

1 Cruiser

The answer to this puzzle
is on page 247.

Battleship Bonanza

puzzle 123

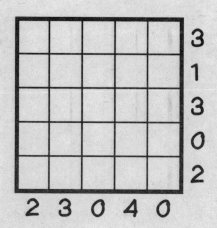

Row clues (top to bottom): 3, 1, 3, 0, 2

Column clues (left to right): 2, 3, 0, 4, 0

2 Submarines

2 Destroyers

1 Cruiser

The answer to this puzzle is on page 247.

Battleship Bonanza

puzzle 124

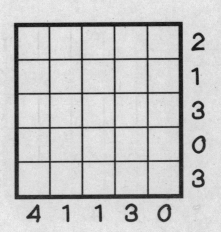

2 Submarines

2 Destroyers

1 Cruiser

The answer to this puzzle
is on page 248.

Battleship Bonanza

puzzle 125

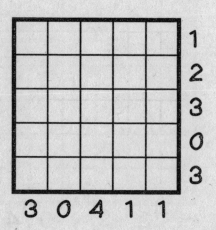

					1
					2
					3
					0
					3
3	0	4	1	1	

2 Submarines

2 Destroyers

1 Cruiser

The answer to this puzzle
is on page 248.

Battleship Bonanza

puzzle 126

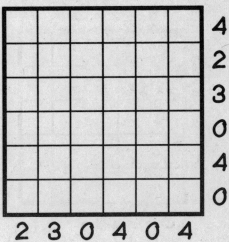

Grid row clues (top to bottom): 4, 2, 3, 0, 4, 0

Grid column clues (left to right): 2, 3, 0, 4, 0, 4

3 Submarines   2 Destroyers

2 Cruisers

The answer to this puzzle
is on page 248.

Battleship Bonanza

puzzle 127

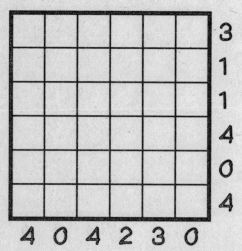

						3
						1
						1
						4
						0
						4

4 0 4 2 3 0

3 Submarines   2 Destroyers

2 Cruisers

The answer to this puzzle
is on page 248.

Battleship Bonanza

puzzle 128

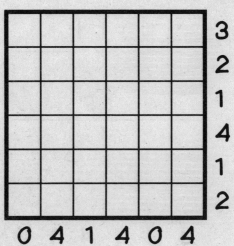

3
2
1
4
1
2

0 4 1 4 0 4

3 Submarines

2 Destroyers

2 Cruisers

The answer to this puzzle is on page 249.

Battleship Bonanza

puzzle 129

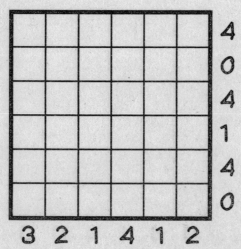

Row numbers (top to bottom): 4, 0, 4, 1, 4, 0

Column numbers (left to right): 3, 2, 1, 4, 1, 2

3 Submarines

2 Destroyers

2 Cruisers

The answer to this puzzle is on page 249.

Battleship Bonanza

puzzle 130

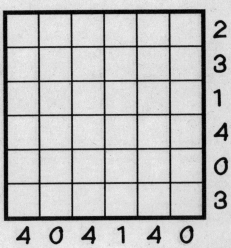

						2
						3
						1
						4
						0
						3
4	0	4	1	4	0	

3 Submarines

2 Destroyers

2 Cruisers

The answer to this puzzle is on page 249.

Battleship Bonanza

puzzle 131

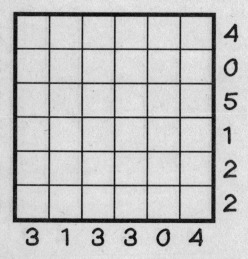

						4
						0
						5
						1
						2
						2

3   1   3   3   0   4

3 Submarines

2 Destroyers

1 Cruiser

1 Battleship

The answer to this puzzle
is on page 249.

Battleship Bonanza

puzzle 132

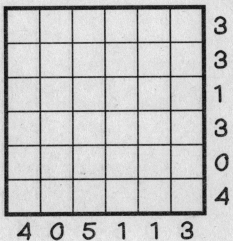

Column totals: 4 0 5 1 1 3

Row totals (top to bottom): 3 3 1 3 0 4

3 Submarines

2 Destroyers

1 Cruiser

1 Battleship

The answer to this puzzle is on page 250.

Battleship Bonanza

puzzle 133

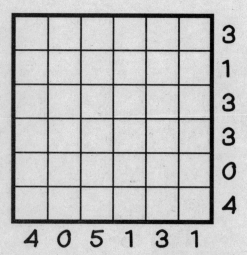

3
1
3
3
0
4

4 0 5 1 3 1

3 Submarines

2 Destroyers

1 Cruiser

1 Battleship

The answer to this puzzle
is on page 250.

178

Battleship
Bonanza

puzzle 134

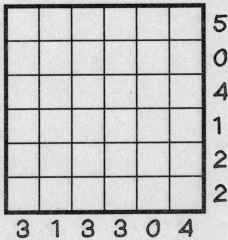

3 Submarines

2 Destroyers

1 Cruiser

1 Battleship

The answer to this puzzle
is on page 250.

Battleship Bonanza

puzzle 135

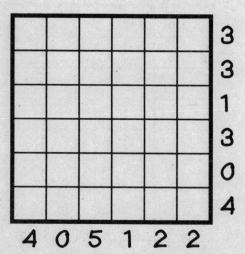

Row clues (top to bottom): 3 3 1 3 0 4

Column clues (left to right): 4 0 5 1 2 2

3 Submarines

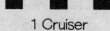

2 Destroyers

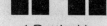

1 Cruiser

1 Battleship

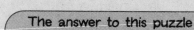

The answer to this puzzle
is on page 250.

Battleship Bonanza

puzzle 136

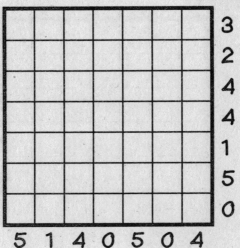

							3
							2
							4
							4
							1
							5
							0
5	1	4	0	5	0	4	

3 Submarines

2 Destroyers

1 Cruiser

1 Battleship

1 Aircraft Carrier

The answer to this puzzle is on page 251.

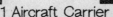

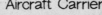

Battleship Bonanza

puzzle 137

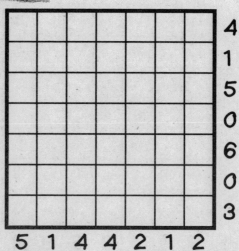

Column totals: 5 1 4 4 2 1 2
Row totals (top to bottom): 4 1 5 0 6 0 3

3 Submarines

2 Destroyers

1 Cruiser

1 Battleship

1 Aircraft Carrier

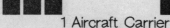

The answer to this puzzle
is on page 251.

Battleship Bonanza

puzzle 138

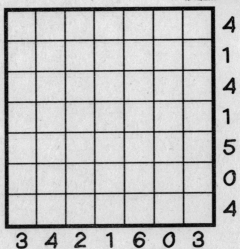

							4
							1
							4
							1
							5
							0
							4
3	4	2	1	6	0	3	

3 Submarines

2 Destroyers

1 Cruiser

1 Battleship

1 Aircraft Carrier

The answer to this puzzle is on page 251.

Battleship Bonanza

puzzle 139

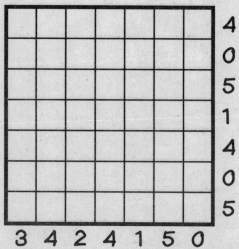

Right side (top to bottom): 4 0 5 1 4 0 5

Bottom (left to right): 3 4 2 4 1 5 0

3 Submarines 2 Destroyers

1 Cruiser  1 Battleship

1 Aircraft Carrier

The answer to this puzzle
is on page 252.

184

Battleship Bonanza

puzzle 140

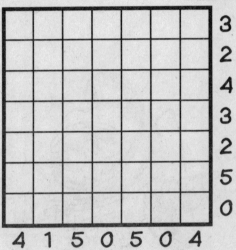

							3
							2
							4
							3
							2
							5
							0

4 1 5 0 5 0 4

3 Submarines

2 Destroyers

1 Cruiser

1 Battleship

1 Aircraft Carrier

The answer to this puzzle
is on page 252.

185

Cosmic Connectors

Cosmic Connectors

Cosmic Connectors look like ordinary crosswords, but they have a twist! Instead of having clues written next to them, all the clues you need are contained within the puzzle — which is cool because it means you don't have to keep looking away.

To complete the puzzle, fill in each empty box with a number from 1 to 9 to make all the sums correct. The sums must work both across and down.

Top Tip: It's easiest to start with a row or column that only has one number missing.

puzzle 141

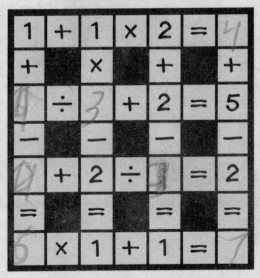

The answer to this puzzle is on page 253.

Cosmic Connectors

puzzle 142

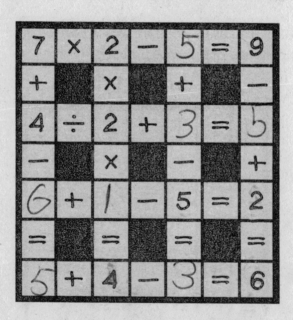

7	×	2	−	5	=	9
+		×		+		−
4	÷	2	+	3	=	5
−		×		−		+
6	+	1	−	5	=	2
=		=		=		=
5	+	4	−	3	=	6

The answer to this puzzle
is on page 253.

Cosmic Connectors

puzzle 143

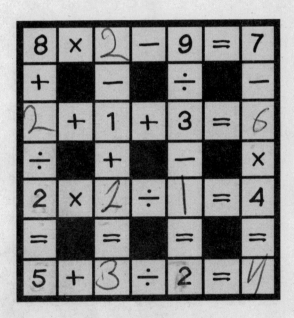

The answer to this puzzle is on page 253.

Cosmic Connectors

puzzle 144

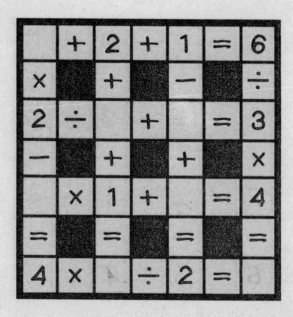

The answer to this puzzle is on page 254.

Cosmic Connectors

puzzle 145

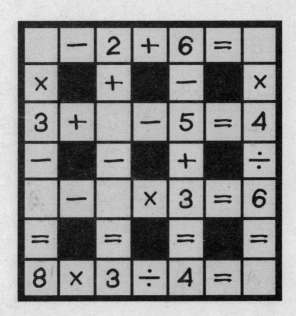

The answer to this puzzle
is on page 254.

Cosmic Connectors

puzzle 146

8	−	5	+		=	7
+		+		+		×
	+		÷	7	=	
−		−		−		−
9	×	2	÷		=	6
=		=		=		=
7	+		−	8	=	

The answer to this puzzle is on page 254.

Cosmic Connectors

puzzle 147

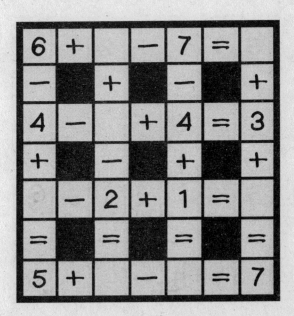

6	+		−	7	=	
−		+		−		+
4	−		+	4	=	3
+		−		+		+
	−	2	+	1	=	
=		=		=		=
5	+		−		=	7

The answer to this puzzle
is on page 255.

Cosmic Connectors

puzzle 148

9	+		÷	2	=	
+		−		÷		÷
	×	6	−		=	4
−		+		+		×
7	−		×	1	=	3
=		=		=		=
	+	5	−		=	6

The answer to this puzzle
is on page 255.

Cosmic Connectors

puzzle 149

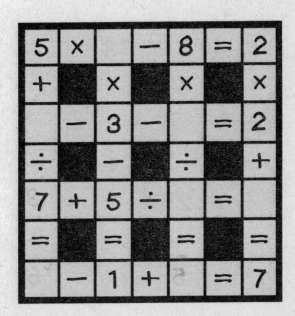

5	×		−	8	=	2
+		×		×		×
	−	3	−		=	2
÷		−		÷		+
7	+	5	÷		=	
=		=		=		=
	−	1	+		=	7

The answer to this puzzle
is on page 255.

Cosmic Connectors

puzzle 150

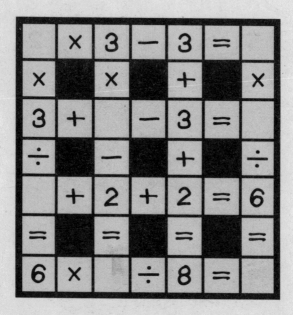

	×	3	−	3	=	
×		×		+		×
3	+		−	3	=	
÷		−		+		÷
	+	2	+	2	=	6
=		=		=		=
6	×		÷	8	=	

The answer to this puzzle
is on page 255.

All the Answers

Daredevil Dominoes

Puzzle 1

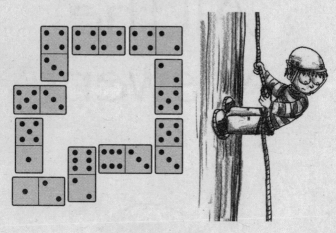

Puzzle 2

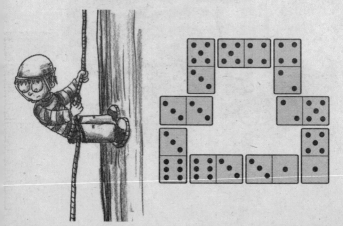

Daredevil Dominoes

Puzzle 3

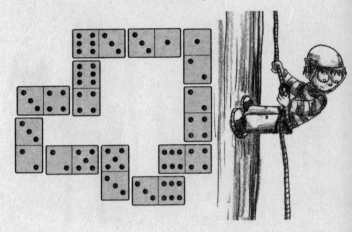

Puzzle 4

Daredevil Dominoes

Puzzle 5

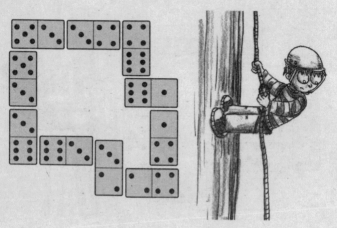

Puzzle 6

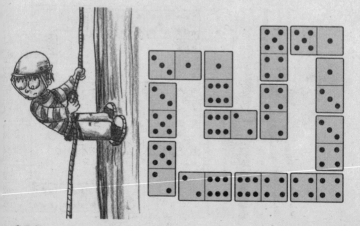

Daredevil Dominoes

Puzzle 7

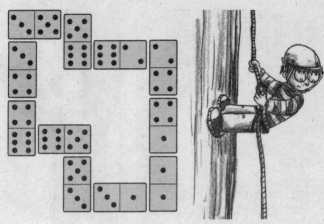

Puzzle 8

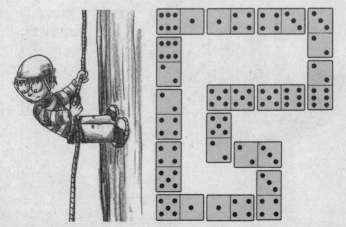

Daredevil Dominoes

Puzzle 9

Puzzle 10

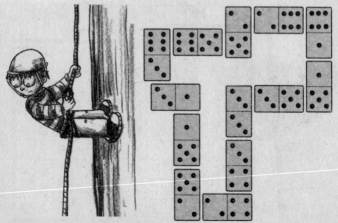

Super-Slammin' Sudoku

7	6	1	2	3	4	8	9	5
8	9	5	6	1	7	3	2	4
4	2	3	5	8	9	1	7	6
9	8	4	1	2	3	5	6	7
5	7	6	9	4	8	2	3	1
3	1	2	7	6	5	4	8	9
6	4	9	8	5	2	7	1	3
2	3	7	4	9	1	6	5	8
1	5	8	3	7	6	9	4	2

Puzzle 11 ➝

5	1	3	2	9	7	6	4	8
8	6	9	1	4	3	5	7	2
7	2	4	6	8	5	3	1	9
4	7	2	5	1	6	9	8	3
6	8	1	7	3	9	4	2	5
9	3	5	4	2	8	1	6	7
2	5	8	3	6	1	7	9	4
1	9	7	8	5	4	2	3	6
3	4	6	9	7	2	8	5	1

⬅ Puzzle 12

1	3	2	5	4	8	7	6	9
6	9	7	2	1	3	5	8	4
5	8	4	9	7	6	2	3	1
3	1	8	6	2	9	4	5	7
2	4	6	7	3	5	1	9	8
7	5	9	1	8	4	6	2	3
8	6	5	4	9	1	3	7	2
9	7	1	3	5	2	8	4	6
4	2	3	8	6	7	9	1	5

Puzzle 13 ➝

Super-Slammin' Sudoku

3	9	6	7	5	1	4	8	2
8	5	7	9	2	4	6	3	1
2	4	1	6	3	8	9	7	5
1	8	5	3	6	9	7	2	4
6	7	3	1	4	2	5	9	8
9	2	4	8	7	5	1	6	3
5	1	8	2	9	7	3	4	6
7	3	2	4	1	6	8	5	9
4	6	9	5	8	3	2	1	7

Puzzle 14 ➜

3	6	9	5	1	4	8	7	2
8	1	5	3	2	7	9	4	6
4	2	7	9	6	8	1	3	5
5	4	6	8	9	2	3	1	7
2	7	3	6	4	1	5	9	8
9	8	1	7	3	5	6	2	4
1	5	8	2	7	3	4	6	9
6	3	2	4	8	9	7	5	1
7	9	4	1	5	6	2	8	3

⬅ Puzzle 15

6	2	4	5	8	1	3	9	7
9	3	1	2	7	6	8	4	5
7	5	8	4	3	9	2	6	1
1	6	7	9	2	3	4	5	8
8	4	5	6	1	7	9	3	2
2	9	3	8	4	5	7	1	6
4	8	6	3	5	2	1	7	9
3	1	9	7	6	8	5	2	4
5	7	2	1	9	4	6	8	3

Puzzle 16 ➜

Super-Slammin' Sudoku

4	1	5	6	9	3	8	2	7
9	2	7	5	1	8	4	6	3
8	3	6	7	4	2	1	9	5
6	5	9	2	7	1	3	4	8
3	8	1	4	6	9	5	7	2
7	4	2	8	3	5	6	1	9
2	9	8	1	5	4	7	3	6
1	7	3	9	8	6	2	5	4
5	6	4	3	2	7	9	8	1

Puzzle 17 ➞

1	9	2	7	6	8	5	4	3
7	5	3	4	2	1	6	8	9
4	6	8	5	9	3	7	1	2
6	4	9	1	5	7	3	2	8
8	2	1	6	3	4	9	5	7
3	7	5	2	8	9	4	6	1
9	1	4	8	7	6	2	3	5
5	3	6	9	1	2	8	7	4
2	8	7	3	4	5	1	9	6

⬅ Puzzle 18

3	1	6	2	5	7	9	8	4
8	7	9	3	4	1	5	6	2
4	5	2	9	6	8	1	7	3
5	2	3	7	1	6	8	4	9
1	4	8	5	3	9	7	2	6
6	9	7	8	2	4	3	5	1
7	3	1	4	8	2	6	9	5
9	6	4	1	7	5	2	3	8
2	8	5	6	9	3	4	1	7

Puzzle 19 ➞

Super-Slammin' Sudoku

8	1	9	4	2	3	7	6	5
5	6	7	8	9	1	2	3	4
2	4	3	7	6	5	1	9	8
1	2	4	6	3	7	5	8	9
3	8	5	9	1	4	6	2	7
7	9	6	2	5	8	3	4	1
4	3	8	5	7	2	9	1	6
6	7	1	3	4	9	8	5	2
9	5	2	1	8	6	4	7	3

Puzzle 20 ➝

1	3	7	5	8	6	9	2	4
4	6	9	3	2	7	8	5	1
2	5	8	9	4	1	7	6	3
3	8	1	2	9	4	6	7	5
7	4	5	1	6	8	3	9	2
9	2	6	7	3	5	4	1	8
5	1	3	8	7	9	2	4	6
6	7	2	4	1	3	5	8	9
8	9	4	6	5	2	1	3	7

⬅ Puzzle 21

4	7	8	6	9	1	5	3	2
3	6	5	8	7	2	1	9	4
1	9	2	4	5	3	6	8	7
9	2	3	1	6	7	4	5	8
5	8	7	2	3	4	9	6	1
6	4	1	5	8	9	2	7	3
8	1	9	7	4	5	3	2	6
2	3	6	9	1	8	7	4	5
7	5	4	3	2	6	8	1	9

Puzzle 22 ➝

Super-Slammin' Sudoku

7	1	3	6	9	5	4	8	2
2	6	4	3	8	1	5	7	9
8	5	9	2	4	7	1	3	6
4	9	6	7	2	3	8	1	5
3	2	8	5	1	9	6	4	7
1	7	5	4	6	8	9	2	3
6	4	7	8	5	2	3	9	1
5	3	1	9	7	4	2	6	8
9	8	2	1	3	6	7	5	4

Puzzle 23 →

6	8	7	9	4	1	5	2	3
2	9	3	6	5	7	1	4	8
5	1	4	3	2	8	7	6	9
8	2	9	5	1	3	6	7	4
7	4	1	2	9	6	8	3	5
3	5	6	7	8	4	9	1	2
4	7	5	8	6	2	3	9	1
1	3	8	4	7	9	2	5	6
9	6	2	1	3	5	4	8	7

← Puzzle 24

1	6	5	2	7	4	8	9	3
9	8	7	1	3	5	2	6	4
3	2	4	9	6	8	5	7	1
7	4	1	6	5	9	3	2	8
5	3	6	4	8	2	9	1	7
2	9	8	3	1	7	6	4	5
4	1	9	8	2	3	7	5	6
6	5	3	7	9	1	4	8	2
8	7	2	5	4	6	1	3	9

Puzzle 25 →

Super-Slammin' Sudoku

3	4	9	7	2	8	1	6	5
5	7	1	3	4	6	8	2	9
6	2	8	9	1	5	7	3	4
7	8	5	6	9	3	2	4	1
4	3	2	5	8	1	9	7	6
9	1	6	4	7	2	5	8	3
2	9	7	1	3	4	6	5	8
1	6	4	8	5	7	3	9	2
8	5	3	2	6	9	4	1	7

Puzzle 26 →

9	7	1	4	8	5	2	6	3
5	2	3	1	7	6	4	9	8
6	8	4	2	3	9	5	1	7
2	1	8	5	4	3	9	7	6
7	6	5	9	1	8	3	4	2
3	4	9	6	2	7	8	5	1
1	9	7	3	5	2	6	8	4
8	3	6	7	9	4	1	2	5
4	5	2	8	6	1	7	3	9

← Puzzle 27

2	9	4	5	3	1	7	8	6
1	7	5	6	9	8	4	2	3
8	6	3	4	2	7	5	9	1
7	4	9	2	8	6	3	1	5
3	5	2	7	1	4	8	6	9
6	1	8	3	5	9	2	4	7
5	8	6	1	4	3	9	7	2
9	2	7	8	6	5	1	3	4
4	3	1	9	7	2	6	5	8

Puzzle 28 →

Super-Slammin' Sudoku

1	4	7	2	9	6	3	5	8
3	6	5	4	7	8	2	1	9
2	9	8	3	5	1	6	4	7
9	7	1	5	3	4	8	6	2
6	8	4	1	2	9	7	3	5
5	3	2	6	8	7	1	9	4
7	1	6	9	4	2	5	8	3
4	2	3	8	1	5	9	7	6
8	5	9	7	6	3	4	2	1

Puzzle 29 ➝

9	6	8	4	5	1	2	3	7
3	2	5	6	9	7	4	1	8
1	7	4	3	2	8	5	6	9
2	8	1	5	6	9	3	7	4
6	9	3	1	7	4	8	2	5
4	5	7	2	8	3	1	9	6
8	3	6	7	1	5	9	4	2
7	4	9	8	3	2	6	5	1
5	1	2	9	4	6	7	8	3

⬅ Puzzle 30

5	7	9	3	8	4	6	2	1
2	1	6	9	7	5	3	4	8
8	4	3	6	2	1	9	5	7
6	2	8	4	9	7	5	1	3
1	9	7	5	3	8	2	6	4
4	3	5	1	6	2	7	8	9
7	5	2	8	1	3	4	9	6
3	6	1	2	4	9	8	7	5
9	8	4	7	5	6	1	3	2

Puzzle 31 ➝

Super-Slammin' Sudoku

Puzzle 32 →

5	8	1	4	2	7	3	6	9
4	2	3	9	5	6	7	1	8
9	7	6	1	3	8	5	4	2
1	6	2	8	9	5	4	3	7
8	3	4	7	1	2	9	5	6
7	9	5	3	6	4	2	8	1
2	4	9	5	8	1	6	7	3
6	1	7	2	4	3	8	9	5
3	5	8	6	7	9	1	2	4

7	1	8	6	2	9	4	3	5
4	3	5	7	8	1	6	2	9
9	6	2	5	4	3	1	7	8
8	9	1	3	5	2	7	6	4
3	5	4	8	7	6	2	9	1
2	7	6	1	9	4	5	8	3
1	2	7	9	3	5	8	4	6
6	4	3	2	1	8	9	5	7
5	8	9	4	6	7	3	1	2

← Puzzle 33

1	6	5	3	2	9	8	7	4
2	7	4	8	5	1	3	6	9
9	8	3	4	6	7	2	1	5
4	1	6	5	3	2	9	8	7
7	3	2	1	9	8	5	4	6
5	9	8	7	4	6	1	2	3
3	2	9	6	8	4	7	5	1
6	5	7	2	1	3	4	9	8
8	4	1	9	7	5	6	3	2

Puzzle 34 →

3	2	4	9	1	5	8	7	6
7	8	6	2	4	3	1	9	5
5	1	9	8	7	6	2	4	3
1	4	3	6	2	9	5	8	7
2	5	8	1	3	7	4	6	9
6	9	7	4	5	8	3	2	1
9	6	1	3	8	4	7	5	2
4	3	5	7	6	2	9	1	8
8	7	2	5	9	1	6	3	4

← Puzzle 35

Nail-Biting Number Searches

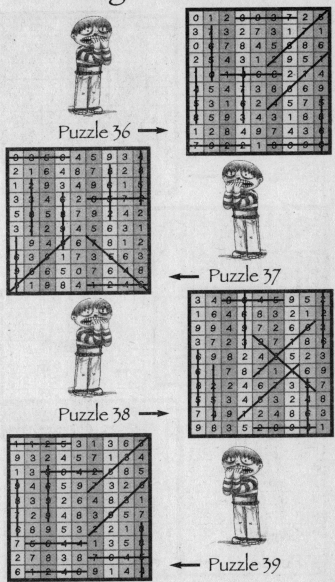

Puzzle 36 →

← Puzzle 37

Puzzle 38 →

← Puzzle 39

211

Nail-Biting Number Searches

Puzzle 40 ➙

0	0	4	5	3	1	4	9	5
5	8	7	3	2	4	6	5	0
2	0	4	3	8	9	7	6	1
1	6	8	6	3	2	2	0	1
2	5	1	4	6	7	8	4	9
4	2	4	8	9	1	5	7	8
9	5	9	4	4	1	1	8	3
8	7	0	2	3	4	5	6	8
1	8	9	8	4	3	9	3	9
9	2	5	7	6	2	5	0	7

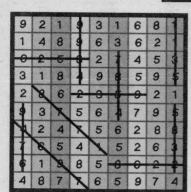

9	2	1	9	3	1	6	8	1
1	4	8	9	6	3	6	2	1
0	2	5	0	2	7	4	5	3
3	1	8	4	9	0	5	9	5
2	0	6	2	0	0	0	2	1
9	3	7	5	6	4	7	9	5
4	2	4	7	5	6	2	8	8
7	6	5	4	1	5	2	6	3
6	1	9	8	5	0	0	2	1
4	8	7	7	6	5	9	7	4

⬅ Puzzle 41

Puzzle 42 ➙

3	2	6	3	6	1	9	8	1
9	4	7	1	4	0	0	7	2
8	7	5	2	1	2	4	5	3
4	2	8	3	5	6	2	8	8
3	2	2	6	1	2	5	5	7
7	3	4	1	0	0	0	0	6
1	8	6	9	7	5	3	4	2
5	1	2	0	5	3	2	9	1
4	8	1	5	9	8	2	1	0
2	9	4	6	9	8	6	5	7

212

Nail-Biting Number Searches

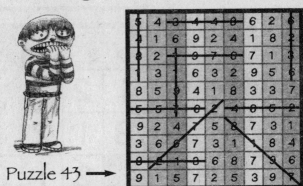

Puzzle 43 ➜

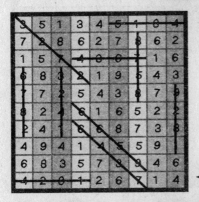

⬅ Puzzle 44

Puzzle 45 ➜

213

Kickin' Kakuro

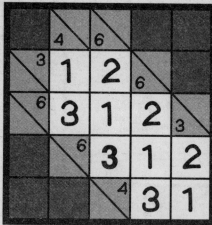

Puzzle 46

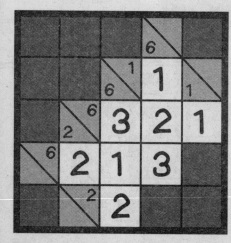

Puzzle 47

Kickin' Kakuro

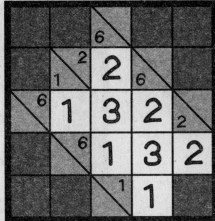

Puzzle 48

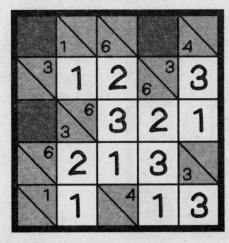

Puzzle 49

Kickin' Kakuro

Puzzle 50

Puzzle 51

Kickin' Kakuro

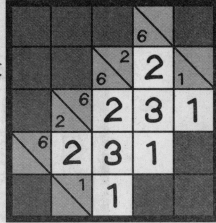

Puzzle 52

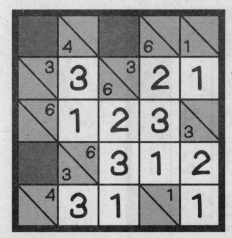

Puzzle 53

Kickin' Kakuro

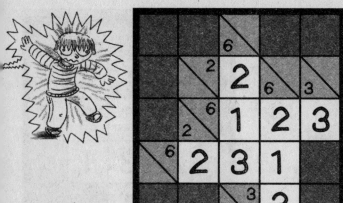

Puzzle 54

Puzzle 55

Kickin' Kakuro

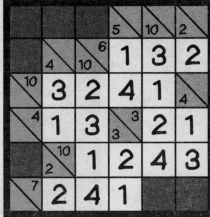

Puzzle 56

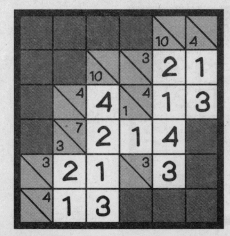

Puzzle 57

Kickin' Kakuro

■	4\	10\	6\	■	■
\6	1	3	2	10\	■
\10	3	2	4	1	■
■	\1	1	3\3	3	4\
■	\10	4	1	2	3
■	■	\7	2	4	1

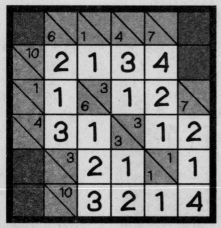

Puzzle 58

■	6\	1\	4\	7\	■
\10	2	1	3	4	■
\1	1	6\3	1	2	7\
\4	3	1	3\3	1	2
■	\3	2	1	1\1	1
■	\10	3	2	1	4

Puzzle 59

Kickin' Kakuro

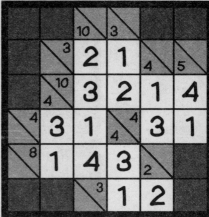

Puzzle 60

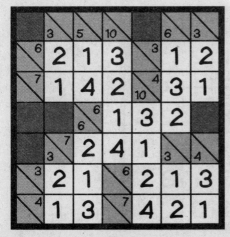

Puzzle 61

Kickin' Kakuro

Puzzle 62

Puzzle 63

Kickin' Kakuro

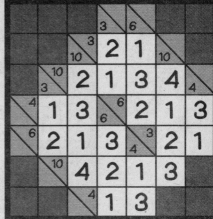

Puzzle 64

Puzzle 65

Kickin' Kakuro

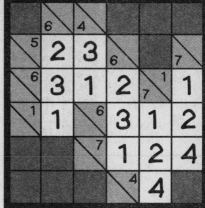

Puzzle 66

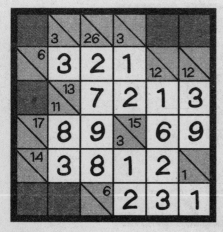

Puzzle 67

224

Kickin' Kakuro

Puzzle 68

Puzzle 68 grid:

	6	1	3	7	11	
15	3	1	2	4	5	
1	1	11/6	1	2	3	
3	2	1	6/3	1	2	7
4	3	1	4/3	1	2	
6	2	3	1	1/1	1	
15	5	2	3	1	4	

Puzzle 69 grid:

	15	3	3				
6	2	3	1	4/7			
3	3	6	2	3	1		15
3	1	2	11/6	1	2	3	5
7	4	1	2	7/3	4	2	1
11	5	3	1	2	4/3	1	3
		6	3	1	2	2/2	2
			7	1	2	4	

Puzzle 69

Puzzle 70

Puzzle 70 grid:

		6	6	13	6	3	3	
23	24	5	6	7	1	3	2	24
4	3	1	5/13	2	3	4/13	1	3
2	2	13/13	7	1	2	3	10/2	2
13	7	1	2	3	10/12	2	7	1
6	1	2	3	13/12	2	1	3	7
6	6	13/5	1	2	3	7	6/5	6
5	4	1	4	3	1	2	2	5
23	4	1	7	6	2	3		

Cool Crossnumbers

Puzzle 71 →

Puzzle 71 grid:

1.1	0	2.1		3.6	3
4		4.2	5.5	0	
6.4	7.9		8.2	0	9.1
	10.3	11.2		0	3
12.3	0	4		13.1	8
3		14.4	15.1	7	
	16.2	5		3	17.1
	1		18.6	0	4

Puzzle 72 grid:

1.7	0	2.2		3.1	6	4.6
2		6		3		4
5.5	0	0	6.5		7.1	0
		8.3	3	0		
9.8	7	10.5		11.7	12.2
	4		13.4	9	0
14.1	0	9		0	
7		15.9	0	2	3

← Puzzle 72

Puzzle 73 →

Puzzle 73 grid:

1.7	4	1	2.5		3.3	2
7			4.5	0	0	
	5.1	2		6.8	7.1
8.7	9.8	6		10.1		0
	3		11.2	8	0
12.1	13.1	4	4			0
14.8	0	0		15.2
	16.6	9		17.4	2

226

Cool Crossnumbers

¹1	²8		³2	7	⁴5
	⁵5	0	0		0
⁶3	0			⁷6	1	6
7			⁸1	0	2
⁹9	0	0	0		¹⁰2
			¹¹1	0	¹²2	4
¹³3	7	¹⁴1			4
5		¹⁵1	8	0	2

Puzzle 74 →

¹5	4		²3	3	³3	3
1		⁴2	4		0
⁵6	⁶4	0	0		⁷1	0	0
	7		⁸2		0
⁹1	6		¹⁰8	¹¹8		¹²8
3				¹³5	6	9
	¹⁴1	0	0	0		1
¹⁵9	7				¹⁶2	5

← Puzzle 75

Puzzle 76 →

¹1	6	²3		³7	6	⁴6
0		⁵5	0	7		0
2				9		0
⁶4	⁷1	0	0	0	
	4				⁸2	3
⁹8	4		¹⁰1		4
4			¹¹1	¹²2	7
¹³6	8	4		4

227

Cool Crossnumbers

Puzzle 77 →

← Puzzle 78

Puzzle 79 →

← Puzzle 80

Hardcore Hanjie

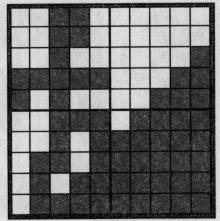

Puzzle 81

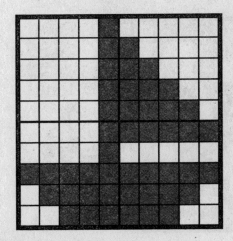

Puzzle 82

Hardcore Hanjie

Puzzle 83

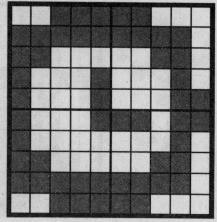

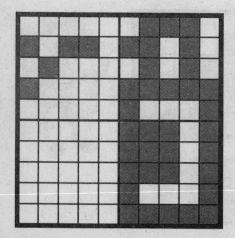

Puzzle 84

Hardcore Hanjie

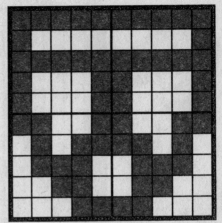

Puzzle 85

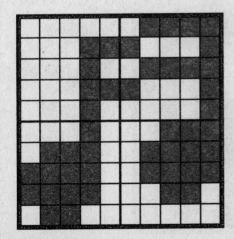

Puzzle 86

Hardcore Hanjie

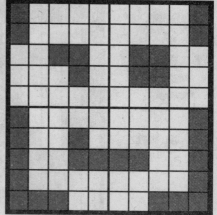

Puzzle 87

Puzzle 88

Hardcore Hanjie

Puzzle 89

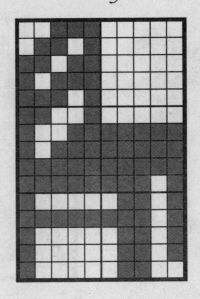

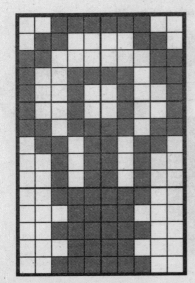

Puzzle 90

Hardcore Hanjie

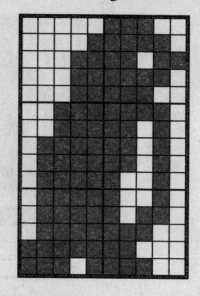

Puzzle 91

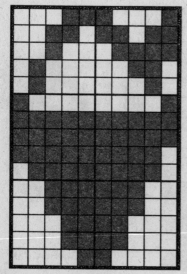

Puzzle 92

Hardcore Hanjie

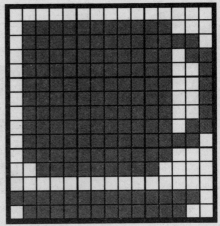

Puzzle 93

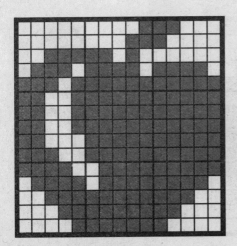

Puzzle 94

Hardcore Hanjie

Puzzle 95

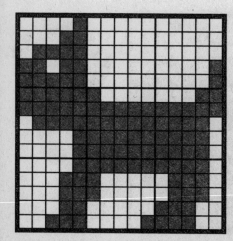

Puzzle 96

Hardcore Hanjie

Puzzle 97

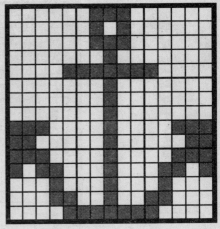

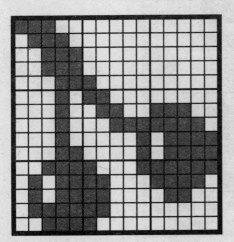

Puzzle 98

Hardcore Hanjie

Puzzle 99

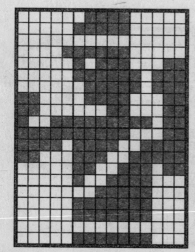

Puzzle 100

Hardcore Hanjie

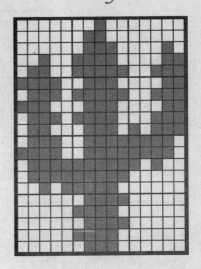

Puzzle 101

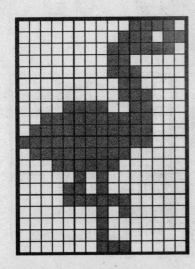

Puzzle 102

Hardcore Hanjie

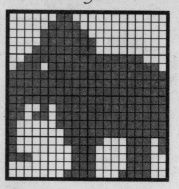

Puzzle 103

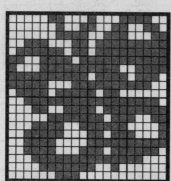

Puzzle 104

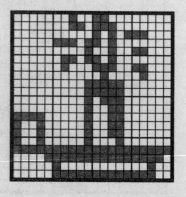

Puzzle 105

Tai-Chi Towers

White Belt

Puzzle 106

Red Belt

Puzzle 107

Tai-Chi Towers

Yellow Belt

	207					
	119	88				
	66	53	35			
	33	33	33	15		
	14	19	14	6	9	
	5	9	10	4	2	7
	3	2	7	3	1	1	6

Puzzle 108

Green Stripe

	268					
	130	138				
	62	68	70			
	30	32	36	34		
	15	15	17	19	15	
	8	7	8	9	10	5
	6	2	5	3	6	4	1

Puzzle 109

Tai-Chi Towers

Green Belt

				522			
			243	279			
		111	132	147			
	50	61	71	76			
21	29	32	39	37			
7	14	16	17	22	15		
2	5	9	7	10	12	3	

Puzzle 110

Blue Stripe

			402			
		198	204			
	106	92	112			
61	45	47	65			
36	25	20	27	35		
19	17	8	12	15	20	
7	12	5	3	9	6	14

Puzzle 111

Tai-Chi Towers

Blue Belt

Puzzle 112

Tower (Puzzle 112):
- 567
- 288, 279
- 155, 133, 146
- 91, 64, 69, 77
- 58, 33, 31, 38, 39
- 36, 22, 11, 20, 18, 21
- 17, 19, 3, 8, 12, 6, 15

Red Stripe

Tower (Puzzle 113):
- 536
- 256, 280
- 128, 128, 152
- 66, 62, 66, 86
- 35, 31, 31, 35, 51
- 20, 15, 16, 15, 20, 31
- 12, 8, 7, 9, 6, 14, 17

Puzzle 113

Tai-Chi Towers

Red Belt

		766		
	416	350		
	222	194	156	
115	107	87	69	
59	56	51	36	33
30	29	27	24	12	21
13	17	12	15	9	3	18

Puzzle 114

Black Belt

843
418 425
197 221 204
89 108 113 91
41 48 60 53 38
20 21 27 33 20 18
7 13 8 19 14 6 12

Puzzle 115

245

Battleship Bonanza

Puzzle 116 →

← Puzzle 117

Puzzle 118 →

← Puzzle 119

Battleship Bonanza

Puzzle 120 →

← Puzzle 121

Puzzle 122 →

← Puzzle 123

247

Battleship Bonanza

Puzzle 124 →

← Puzzle 125

Puzzle 126 →

← Puzzle 127

Battleship Bonanza

Puzzle 128 →

← Puzzle 129

Puzzle 130 →

← Puzzle 131

249

Battleship Bonanza

Puzzle 132 →

← Puzzle 133

Puzzle 134 →

← Puzzle 135

Battleship Bonanza

Puzzle 136 →

← Puzzle 137

Puzzle 138 →

Battleship Bonanza

Puzzle 139 ⟶

⟵ Puzzle 140

Cosmic Connectors

1	+	1	×	2	=	4
+		×		+		+
9	÷	3	+	2	=	5
−		−		−		−
4	+	2	÷	3	=	2
=		=		=		=
6	×	1	+	1	=	7

Puzzle 141 ➞

7	×	2	−	5	=	9
+		×		+		−
4	÷	2	+	3	=	5
−		×		−		+
6	+	1	−	5	=	2
=		=		=		=
5	+	4	−	3	=	6

◀— Puzzle 142

8	×	2	−	9	=	7
+		−		÷		−
2	+	1	+	3	=	6
÷		+		−		×
2	×	2	÷	1	=	4
=		=		=		=
5	+	3	÷	2	=	4

Puzzle 143 ➞

Cosmic Connectors

3	+	2	+	1	=	6
×		+		−		÷
2	÷	1	+	1	=	3
−		+		+		×
2	×	1	+	2	=	4
=		=		=		=
4	×	4	÷	2	=	8

Puzzle 144 ➡

5	−	2	+	6	=	9
×		+		−		×
3	+	6	−	5	=	4
−		−		+		÷
7	−	5	×	3	=	6
=		=		=		=
8	×	3	÷	4	=	6

⬅ Puzzle 145

8	−	5	+	4	=	7
+		+		+		×
8	+	6	÷	7	=	2
−		−		−		−
9	×	2	÷	3	=	6
=		=		=		=
7	+	9	−	8	=	8

Puzzle 146 ➡

254

Cosmic Connectors

Puzzle 147 →

6	+	3	−	7	=	2
−		+		−		+
4	−	5	+	4	=	3
+		−		+		+
3	−	2	+	1	=	2
=		=		=		
5	+	6	−	4	=	7

9	+	7	÷	2	=	8
+		−		÷		÷
1	×	6	−	2	=	4
−		+		+		×
7	−	4	×	1	=	3
=		=		=		
3	+	5	−	2	=	6

← **Puzzle 148**

5	×	2	−	8	=	2
+		×		×		×
9	−	3	−	3	=	2
÷		−		÷		+
7	+	5	÷	4	=	3
=		=		=		
2	−	1	+	6	=	7

Puzzle 149 →

4	×	3	−	3	=	9
×		×		+		×
3	+	2	−	3	=	2
÷		−		+		÷
2	+	2	+	2	=	6
=		=		=		
6	×	4	÷	8	=	3

← **Puzzle 150**

255